Oscar Fingal O'Flahertie Wills Wilde (16 October 1854 – 30 November 1900) was an Irish poet and playwright. After writing in different forms throughout the 1880s, he became one of London's most popular playwrights in the early 1890s. He is best remembered for his epigrams and plays, his novel The Picture of Dorian Gray, and the circumstances of his criminal conviction for homosexuality, imprisonment, and early death at age 46. Wilde's parents were successful Anglo-Irish intellectuals in Dublin. Their son became fluent in French and German early in life. At university, Wilde read Greats; he proved himself to be an outstanding classicist, first at Trinity College Dublin, then at Oxford. He became known for his involvement in the rising philosophy of aestheticism, led by two of his tutors, Walter Pater and John Ruskin. After university, Wilde moved to London into fashionable cultural and social circles. (Source: Wikipedia)

Literary works:
Ravenna (1878)
Poems (1881)
The Happy Prince and Other Stories (1888)
Lord Arthur Savile's Crime and Other Stories (1891)
A House of Pomegranates (1891)
Intentions (1891)
The Picture of Dorian Gray (1890)
The Soul of Man under Socialism (1891)
Lady Windermere's Fan (1892)
A Woman of No Importance (1893)
An Ideal Husband (1898)
The Importance of Being Earnest (1898)
De Profundis (1905)
The Ballad of Reading Gaol (1898)
The Portrait of Mr. W. H. (1889)

SEBASTIAN MELMOTH
&
SELECTED POEMS OF
OSCAR WILDE
INCLUDING THE BALLAD OF READING GAOL

OSCAR WILDE

PRINCE CLASSICS

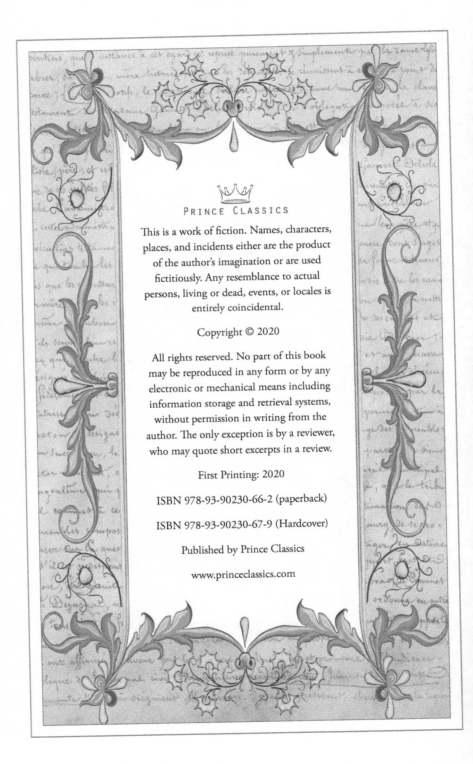

PRINCE CLASSICS

This is a work of fiction. Names, characters, places, and incidents either are the product of the author's imagination or are used fictitiously. Any resemblance to actual persons, living or dead, events, or locales is entirely coincidental.

Copyright © 2020

First Printing: 2020

ISBN 978-93-90230-66-2 (paperback)

ISBN 978-93-90230-67-9 (Hardcover)

Published by Prince Classics

www.princeclassics.com

Contents

SEBASTIAN MELMOTH
&
SELECTED POEMS OF
OSCAR WILDE
INCLUDING THE BALLAD OF READING GAOL

SEBASTIAN MELMOTH

SEBASTIAN MELMOTH
(OSCAR WILDE)

The mystery of love is greater than the mystery of death.

Women are made to be loved, not to be understood.

It is absurd to have a hard and fast rule about what one should read and what one shouldn't. Moren than half of modern culture depends on what one shouldn't read.

Women, as someone says, love with their ears, just as men love with their eyes, if they ever love at all.

It is better to be beautiful than to be good, but it is better to be good than to be ugly.

Nothing looks so like innocence as an indiscretion.

Misfortunes one can endure, they come from outside, they are accidents. But to suffer for one's faults—ah! there is the sting of life.

Beauty is the only thing that time cannot harm. Philosophies fall away like sand, creeds follow one another, but what is beautiful is a joy for all seasons, a possession for all eternity.

Questions are never indiscreet; answers sometimes are.

Twenty years of romance make a woman look like a ruin; but twenty years of marriage make her something like a public building.

The only thing that one really knows about human nature is that it changes.

Anyone can sympathise with the sufferings of a friend, but it requires a very fine nature to sympathise with a friend's success.

Selfishness is not living as one wishes to live, it is asking others to live as one wishes to live: and unselfishness is letting other people's lives alone, not interfering with them.

A man who does not think for himself does not think at all.

Nowadays people seem to look on life as a speculation. It is not a speculation. It is a sacrament. Its ideal is love. Its purification is sacrifice.

In old days nobody pretended to be a bit better than his neighbour. In fact, to be a bit better than one's neighbour was considered excessively vulgar and middle class. Nowadays, with our modern mania for morality, everyone has to pose as a paragon of purity, incorruptibility, and all the other seven deadly virtues. And what is the result? You all go over like ninepins—one after the other.

All sympathy is fine, but sympathy with suffering is the least fine mode.

If you pretend to be good the world takes you very seriously. If you pretend to be bad it doesn't. Such is the astounding stupidity of optimism.

It is most dangerous nowadays for a husband to pay any attention to his wife in public. It always makes people think that he beats her when they're alone. The world has grown so suspicious of anything that looks like a happy married life.

Actors are so fortunate. They can choose whether they will appear in tragedy or in comedy, whether they will suffer or make merry, laugh or shed tears. But in real life it is different. Most men and women are forced to perform parts for which they have no qualifications. The world is a stage, but the play is badly cast.

Men know life too early; women know life too late-that is the difference between men and women.

He who stands most remote from his age is he who mirrors it best.

There is only one thing in the world worse than being talked about, and that is not being talked about.

Life is not governed by will or intention. Life is a question of nerves and fibres and slowly built-up cells, in which thought hides itself and passion has its dreams.

Man is a being with myriad lives and myriad sensations, a complex, multiform creature that bears within itself strange legacies of thought and passion, and whose very flesh is tainted with the monstrous maladies of the dead.

As long as a woman can look ten years younger than her own daughter she is perfectly satisfied.

There is always something infinitely mean about other people's tragedies.

Public and private life are different things. They have different laws and move on different lines.

When one is placed in the position of guardian one has to adopt a very high moral tone on all subjects. It's one's duty to do so.

I have always been of opinion that a man who desires to get married should know either everything or nothing.

An engagement should come on a young girl as a surprise, pleasant or unpleasant, as the case may be. It is hardly a matter that she could be allowed to arrange for herself.

If the lower classes don't set us a good example what on earth is the use of them? They seem, as a class, to have absolutely no sense of moral responsibility.

If a woman cannot make her mistakes charming she is only a female.

The world was made for men and not for women.

It is always with the best intentions that the worst work is done.

If you wish to understand others you must intensify your own individualism.

Why do you talk so trivially about life? Because I think that life is far too important a thing ever to talk seriously about it.

What a pity that in life we only get our lessons when they are of no use to us.

It is better to have a permanent income than to be fascinating.

Relations are simply a tedious pack of people who haven't got the remotest knowledge of how to live nor the smallest instinct about when to die.

Charity creates a multitude of sins.

My experience is that as soon as people are old enough to know better they don't know anything at all.

Truth is a very complex thing and politics is a very complex business. There are wheels within wheels. One may be under certain obligations to people that one must pay. Sooner or later in political life one has to compromise. Everyone does.

Men can love what is beneath them—things unworthy, stained, dishonoured. We women worship when we love; and when we lose our worship we lose everything.

The proper basis for marriage is a mutual misunderstanding.

The one advantage of playing with fire is that one never gets even singed. It is the people who don't know how to play with it who get burned up.

There are moments when one has to choose between living one's own life fully, entirely, completely, or dragging out some false, shallow, degrading existence that the world in its hypocrisy demands.

When one is in town one amuses oneself. When one is in the country one amuses other people. It is excessively boring.

Romance is the privilege of the rich, not the profession of the unemployed. The poor should be practical and prosaic.

An acquaintance that begins with a compliment is sure to develop into a real friendship. It starts in the right manner.

The truths of metaphysics are the truths of masks.

Science can never grapple with the irrational. That is why it has no future before it in this world.

The happy people of the world have their value, but only the negative value of foils. They throw up and emphasise the beauty and the fascination of the unhappy.

In this world there are only two tragedies. One is not getting what one wants, and the other is getting it. The last is much the worst—the last is a real tragedy.

Disobedience in the eyes of anyone who has read history is man's original virtue. It is through disobedience that progress has been made—through disobedience and rebellion.

It is not wise to find symbols in everything that one sees. It makes life too full of terrors.

Comfort is the only thing our civilisation can give us.

Politics are my only pleasure. You see nowadays it is not fashionable to flirt till one is forty or to be romantic till one is forty-five, so we poor women who are under thirty, or say we are, have nothing open to us but politics or philanthropy. And philanthropy seems to me to have become simply the refuge of people who wish to annoy their fellow-creatures. I prefer politics. I think they are more ... becoming.

One's past is what one is. It is the only way by which people should be judged.

In a very ugly and sensible age the arts borrow, not from life, but from each other.

It is always a silly thing to give advice, but to give good advice is fatal.

Secrets from other people's wives are a necessary luxury in modern life.

15

So, at least, I am told at the club by people who are bald enough to know better. But no man should have a secret from his own wife. She invariably finds it out. Women have a wonderful instinct about things. They discover everything except the obvious.

Life holds the mirror up to art, and either reproduces some strange type imagined by painter or sculptor or realises in fact what has been dreamed in fiction.

I feel sure that if I lived in the country for six months I should become so unsophisticated that no one would take the slightest notice of me.

To recommend thrift to the poor is both grotesque and insulting. It is like advising a man who is starving to eat less.

A thing is not necessarily true because a man dies for it.

I am always saying what I shouldn't say; in fact, I usually say what I really think—a great mistake nowadays. It makes one so liable to be misunderstood.

Experience is the name everyone gives to their mistakes.

The true perfection of man lies, not in what man has, but in what man is.

The basis of every scandal is an absolute immoral certainty.

People talk so much about the beauty of confidence. They seem to entirely ignore the much more subtle beauty of doubt. To believe is very dull. To doubt is intensely engrossing. To be on the alert is to live, to be lulled into security is to die.

Every effect that one produces gives one an enemy. To be popular one must be a mediocrity.

It is a sad truth, but we have lost the faculty of giving lovely names to things. Names are everything. I never quarrel with actions, my one quarrel is with words. That is the reason I hate vulgar realism in literature. The man who could call a spade a spade should be compelled to use one. It is the only thing he is fit for.

16

A high moral tone can hardly be said to conduce very much to either one's health or one's happiness.

There are terrible temptations that it requires strength—strength and courage—to yield to. To stake all one's life on one throw—whether the stake be power or pleasure I care not—there is no weakness in that. There is a horrible, a terrible, courage.

Nowadays it is only the unreadable that occurs.

All charming people are spoiled. It is the secret of their attraction.

There is more to be said for stupidity than people imagine. Personally, I have a great admiration for stupidity. It is a sort of fellow-feeling, I suppose.

All men are monsters. The only thing to do is to feed the wretches well. A good cook does wonders.

There is no such thing as an omen.

Destiny does not send us heralds. She is too wise or too cruel for that.

Crying is the refuge of plain women but the ruin of pretty ones.

Love art for its own sake and then all things that you need will be added to you. This devotion to beauty and to the creation of beautiful things is the test of all great civilisations; it is what makes the life of each citizen a sacrament and not a speculation.

It is always worth while asking a question, though it is not always answering one.

It takes a thoroughly good woman to do a thoroughly stupid thing.

With a proper background women can do anything.

Chiromancy is a most dangerous science, and one that ought not to be encouraged, except in a 'tête-à-tête.'

One should never take sides in anything. Taking sides is the beginning of sincerity, and earnestness follows shortly afterwards, and the human being becomes a bore.

The work of art is beautiful by being what art never has been; and to measure it by the standard of the past is to measure it by a standard on the reflection of which its real perfection depends.

There are three kinds of despots. There is the despot who tyrannises over the body. There is the despot who tyrannises over the soul. There is the despot who tyrannises over soul and body alike. The first is called the prince. The second is called the pope. The third is called the people.

Costume is a growth, an evolution, and a most important, perhaps the most important, sign of the manners, customs, and mode of life of each century.

I really don't see anything romantic in proposing. It is very romantic to be in love, but there is nothing romantic about a definite proposal. Why, one may be accepted. One usually is, I believe. Then the excitement is all over. The very essence of romance is uncertainty.

What consoles one nowadays is not repentance but pleasure. Repentance is quite out of date.

Ideals are dangerous things. Realities are better. They wound, but they are better.

Unless one is wealthy there is no use in being a charming fellow.

Shallow sorrows and shallow loves live on. The loves and sorrows that are great are destroyed by their own plenitude.

An eternal smile is much more wearisome than a perpetual frown. The one sweeps away all possibilities, the other suggests a thousand.

To disagree with three-fourths of England on all points is one of the first elements of vanity, which is a deep source of consolation in all moments of spiritual doubt.

Women live by their emotions and for them, they have no philosophy of life.

As long as war is regarded as wicked it will always have a fascination. When it is looked upon as vulgar it will cease to be popular.

There is only one thing worse than injustice, and that is justice without her sword in her hand. When right is not might it is evil.

We spend our days, each one of us, in looking for the secret of life. Well, the secret of life is in art.

The truth isn't quite the sort of thing that one tells to a nice, sweet, refined girl.

If one plays good music people don't listen, and if one plays bad music people don't talk.

How fond women are of doing dangerous things. It is one of the qualities in them that I admire most. A woman will flirt with anybody in the world as long as other people are looking on.

Englishwomen conceal their feelings till after they are married. They show them then.

Moderation is a fatal thing. Nothing succeeds like excess.

Actions are the first tragedy in life, words are the second. Words are perhaps the worst. Words are merciless.

Life is terrible. It rules us, we do not rule it.

In art there is no such thing as a universal truth. A truth in art is that whose contradictory is also true.

One's days are too brief to take the burden of another's sorrows on one's shoulders. Each man lives his own life, and pays his own price for living it. The only pity is that one has to pay so often for a single fault. One has to pay over and over again, indeed. In her dealings with man Destiny never closes her accounts.

Pleasure is Nature's test, her sign of approval. When we are happy we are always good, but when we are good we are not always happy.

19

The people who love only once in their lives are really the shallow people. What they call their loyalty and their fidelity I call either the lethargy of custom or their lack of imagination.

Better to take pleasure in a rose than to put its root under a microscope.

Of Shakespeare it may be said that he was the first to see the dramatic value of doublets and that a climax may depend on a crinoline.

Plain women are always jealous of their husbands; beautiful women never are! They never have time. They are always so occupied in being jealous of other people's husbands.

What between the duties expected of one during one's lifetime and the duties exacted from one after one's death land has ceased to be either a profit or a pleasure. It gives one position and prevents one from keeping it up.

A man who moralises is usually a hypocrite, and a woman who moralises is invariably plain. There is nothing in the whole world so unbecoming to a woman as a nonconformist conscience. And most women know it, I am glad to say.

It was a fatal day when the public discovered that the pen is mightier than the paving-stone and can be made as offensive as a brickbat.

A map of the world that does not include Utopia is not worth even glancing at, for it leaves out the one country at which Humanity is always landing. And when Humanity lands there it looks out, and, seeing a better country, sets sail. Progress is the realisation of Utopias.

What is the difference between scandal and gossip? Oh! gossip is charming! History is merely gossip, but scandal is gossip made tedious by morality.

All beautiful things belong to the same age.

It is personalities, not principles, that move the age.

Modern pictures are, no doubt, delightful to look at. At least, some of them are. But they are quite impossible to live with; they are too clever, too assertive, too intellectual. Their meaning is too obvious and their method too clearly defined. One exhausts what they have to say in a very short time, and then they become as tedious as one's relations.

To know nothing about our great men is one of the necessary elements of English education.

The truth is rarely pure and never simple. Modern life would be very tedious if it were either and modern literature a complete impossibility.

You may laugh, but it is a great thing to come across a woman who thoroughly understands one.

The majority of people spoil their lives by an unhealthy and exaggerated altruism.

The number of women in London who flirt with their own husbands is perfectly scandalous. It looks so bad. It is simply washing one's clean linen in public.

The chief thing that makes life a failure from the artistic point of view is the thing that lends to life its sordid security—the fact that one can never repeat exactly the same emotion.

We teach people how to remember, we never teach them how to grow.

Vulgar habit that is people have nowadays of asking one, after one has given them an idea, whether one is serious or not. Nothing is serious except passion. The intellect is not a serious thing and never has been. It is an instrument on which one plays, that is all. The only serious form of intellect I know is the British intellect, and on the British intellect the illiterate always plays the drum.

It is absurd to divide people into good and bad. People are either charming or tedious.

It is only the modern that ever become old-fashioned.

It is only the Philistine who seeks to estimate a personality by the vulgar test of production.

Musical people are so absurdly unreasonable. They always want one to be perfectly dumb at the very moment when one is longing to be absolutely deaf.

Nothing is so dangerous as being too modern. One is apt to grow old-fashioned quite suddenly.

The fact of a man being a poisoner is nothing against his prose. The domestic virtues are not the true basis of art.

To the philosopher women represent the triumph of matter over mind, just as men represent the triumph of mind over morals.

The only way a woman can ever reform a man is by boring him so completely that he loses all possible interest in life.

The only horrible thing in the world is 'ennui.' That is the one sin for which there is no forgiveness.

French songs I cannot possibly allow. People always seem to think that they are improper, and either look shocked, which is vulgar, or laugh, which is worse.

It has often been made a subject of reproach against artists and men of letters that they are lacking in wholeness and completeness of nature. As a rule this must necessarily be so. That very concentration of vision and inversity of purpose which is the characteristic of the artistic temperament is in itself a mode of limitation. To those who are preoccupied with the beauty of form nothing else seems of so much importance.

The work of art is to dominate the spectator. The spectator is not to dominate the work of art.

One should sympathise with the joy, the beauty, the colour of life. The less said about life's sores the better.

You can't make people good by act of Parliament—that is something.

Art creates an incomparable and unique effect, and having done so passes on to other things. Nature, on the other hand, forgetting that imitation can be made the sincerest form of insult, keeps on repeating the effect until we all become absolutely wearied of it.

It is perfectly monstrous the way people go about nowadays saying things against one behind one's back that are absolutely and entirely true.

A true artist takes no notice whatever of the public. The public are to him non-existent.

One should never trust a woman who tells one her real age. A woman who would tell one that would tell one anything.

Nothing is so aggravating as calmness. There is something positively brutal about the good temper of most modern men. I wonder we women stand it as well as we do.

The truth is a thing I get rid of as soon as possible. Bad habit, by the way, makes one very unpopular at the club ... with the older members. They call it being conceited. Perhaps it is.

My own business always bores me to death. I prefer other people's.

Don't be led astray into the paths of virtue—that is the worst of women. They always want one to be good. And if we are good, when they meet us they don't love us at all. They like to find us quite irretrievably bad and to leave us quite unattractively good.

Men are such cowards. They outrage every law in the world and are afraid of the world's tongue.

Wicked women bother one. Good women bore one. That is the only difference between them.

To know the principles of the highest art is to know the principles of all the arts.

I don't believe in the existence of Puritan women. I don't think there is a woman in the world who would not be a little flattered if one made love to her. It is that which makes women so irresistibly adorable.

When I am in trouble eating is the only thing that consoles me. Indeed, when I am in really great trouble, as anyone who knows me intimately will tell you, I refuse everything except food and drink.

When one is going to lead an entirely new life one requires regular and wholesome meals.

The soul is born old, but grows young. That is the comedy of life. The body is born young, and grows old. That is life's tragedy.

One can survive everything nowadays except death, and live down anything except a good reputation.

The past is of no importance. The present is of no importance. It is with the future that we have to deal. For the past is what men should not have been. The present is what men ought not to be. The future is what artists are.

Men become old, but they never become good.

By persistently remaining single a man converts himself into a permanent public temptation. Men should be more careful; this very celibacy leads weaker vessels astray.

I think that in practical life there is something about success, actual success, that is a little unscrupulous, something about ambition that is scrupulous always.

Every man of ambition has to fight his century with its own weapons. What this century worships is wealth. The god of this century is wealth. To succeed one must have wealth. At all costs one must have wealth.

I love scandals about other people, but scandals about myself don't interest me. They have not got the charm of novelty.

Moderation is a fatal thing. Enough is as bad as a meal. More than enough is as good as a feast.

The English can't stand a man who is always saying he is in the right, but they are very fond of a man who admits he has been in the wrong. It is one of the best things in them.

Life is simply a 'mauvais quart d'heure' made up of exquisite moments.

24

There is the same world for all of us, and good and evil, sin and innocence, go through it hand in hand. To shut one's eyes to half of life that one may live securely is as though one blinded oneself that one might walk with more safety in a land of pit and precipice.

Married men are horribly tedious when they are good husbands and abominably conceited when they are not.

Between men and women there is no friendship possible. There is passion, enmity, worship, love, but no friendship.

Everybody is clever nowadays. You can't go anywhere without meeting clever people. This has become an absolute public nuisance.

I don't think man has much capacity for development. He has got as far as he can, and that is not far, is it?

I am not quite sure that I quite know what pessimism really means. All I do know is that life cannot be understood without much charity, cannot be lived without much charity. It is love, and not German philosophy, that is the explanation of this world, whatever may be the explanation of the next.

I do not approve of anything that that tampers with natural arrogance. Ignorance is like a delicate exotic fruit: touch it, and the blossom is gone.

The whole theory of modern education is radically unsound. Fortunately, in England, at any rate, education produces no effect whatsoever. If it did it would prove a serious danger to the upper classes, and probably lead to acts of violence in Grosvenor Square.

No woman should ever be quite accurate about her age. It looks so calculating.

Emotion for the sake of emotion is the aim of art, and emotion for the sake of emotion is the aim of life and of that practical organisation of life that we call society.

Men of the noblest possible moral character are extremely susceptible to the influence of the physical charms of others. Modern, no less than ancient, history supplies us with many most painful examples of what I refer to. If it were not so, indeed, history would be quite unreadable.

I am not in favour of long engagements. They give people the opportunity of finding out each other's character before marriage, which I think is never advisable.

It is a terrible thing for a man to find out suddenly that all his life he has been speaking nothing but the truth.

The two weak points in our age are its want of principle and its want of profile.

Thirty-five is a very attractive age. London society is full of women who have of their own free choice remained thirty-five for years.

Never speak disrespectfully of society. Only people who can't get into it do that.

It is always painful to part with people whom one has known for a very brief space of time. The absence of old friends one can endure with equanimity. But even a momentary separation from anyone to whom one has just been introduced is almost unbearable.

To be natural is to be obvious, and to be obvious is to be inartistic.

One is tempted to define man as a rational animal who always loses his temper when he is called upon to act in accordance with the dictates of reason.

The essence of thought, as the essence of life, is growth.

What people call insincerity is simply a method by which we can multiply our personalities.

In a temple everyone should be serious except the thing that is worshipped.

We are never more true to ourselves than when we are inconsistent.

There is always something ridiculous about the emotions of people whom one has ceased to love.

Intellectual generalities are always interesting, but generalities in morals mean absolutely nothing.

To be in society is merely a bore, but to be out of it simply a tragedy.

We live in an age when unnecessary things are our only necessities.

One should never make one's début with a scandal. One should reserve that to give an interest to one's old age.

What man has sought for is, indeed, neither pain nor pleasure, but simply life. Man has sought to live intensely, fully, perfectly. When he can do so without exercising restraint on others, or suffering it ever, and his activities are all pleasurable to him, he will be saner, healthier, more civilised, more himself. Pleasure is nature's test, her sign of approval. When man is happy he is in harmony with himself and his environment.

Society often forgives the criminal, it never forgives the dreamer.

It is so easy for people to have sympathy with suffering. It is so difficult for them to have sympathy with thought.

Conversation should touch on everything, but should concentrate itself on nothing.

There is a luxury in self-reproach. When we blame ourselves we feel that no one else has a right to blame us. It is the confession, not the priest, that gives us absolution.

There are only two kinds of people who are really fascinating—people who know absolutely everything and people who know absolutely nothing.

The public is wonderfully tolerant; it forgives everything except genius.

Life makes us pay too high a price for its wares, and we purchase the meanest of its secrets at a cost that is monstrous and infinite.

This horrid House of Commons quite ruins our husbands for us. I think the Lower House by far the greatest blow to a happy married life that there has been since that terrible thing they called the Higher Education of Women was invented.

Once a man begins to neglect his domestic duties he becomes painfully effeminate, does he not? And I don't like that. It makes men so very attractive.

Experience is a question of instinct about life.

What is true about art is true about life.

One can always be kind to people about whom one cares nothing.

I like men who have a future and women who have a past.

Women, as some witty Frenchman put it, inspire us with the desire to do masterpieces and always prevent us from carrying them out.

In matters of grave importance style, not sincerity, is the vital thing.

The only way to behave to a woman, is to make love to her if she is pretty and to someone else if she is plain.

Women give to men the very gold of their lives. Possibly; but they invariably want it back in such very small change.

Define women as a sex? Sphinxes without secrets.

What do you call a bad man? The sort of man who admires innocence.

What do you call a bad woman? Oh! the sort of woman a man never gets tired of.

One can resist everything except temptation.

Don't let us go to life for our fulfilment or our experience. It is a thing narrowed by circumstances, incoherent in its utterance, and without that fine correspondence or form and spirit which is the only thing that can satisfy the artistic and critical temperament.

It is a dangerous thing to reform anyone.

One can always know at once whether a man has home claims upon his life or not. I have noticed a very, very sad expression in the eyes of so many married men.

A mother who doesn't part with a daughter every season has no real affection.

To be good is to be in harmony with oneself. Discord is to be forced to be in harmony with others.

A really grand passion is comparatively rare nowadays. It is the privilege of people who have nothing to do. That is the one use of the idle classes in a country.

There is no secret of life. Life's aim, if it has one, is simply to be always looking for temptations. There are not nearly enough of them; I sometimes pass a whole day without coming across a single one. It is quite dreadful. It makes one so nervous about the future.

All thought is immoral. Its very essence is destruction. If you think of anything you kill it; nothing survives being thought of.

What is truth? In matters of religion it is simply the opinion that has survived. In matters of science it is the ultimate sensation. In matters of art it is one's last mood.

It is so easy to convert others. It is so difficult to convert oneself.

A little sincerity is a dangerous thing, and a great deal of it is absolutely fatal.

Life cheats us with shadows, like a puppet-master. We ask it for pleasure. It gives it to us, with bitterness and disappointment in its train. We come across some noble grief that we think will lend the purple dignity of tragedy to our days, but it passes away from us, and things less noble take its place, and on some grey, windy dawn, or odorous eve of silence and of silver, we find ourselves looking with callous wonder, or dull heart of stone, at the tress of gold-flecked hair that we had once so wildly worshipped and so madly kissed.

There are two ways of disliking art One is to dislike it and the other to

29

like it rationally.

There is nothing sane about the worship of beauty. It is too splendid to be sane. Those of whose lives it forms the dominant note will always seem to the world to be mere visionaries.

I am afraid that good people do a great deal of harm in this world. Certainly the greatest harm they do is that they make badness of such extraordinary importance.

A sentimentalist is a man who sees an absurd value in everything and doesn't know the marked price of any single thing.

Punctuality is the thief of time.

Self-culture is the true ideal for man.

There's nothing in the world like the devotion of a married woman. It's a thing no married man knows anything about.

No woman should have a memory. Memory in a woman is the beginning of dowdiness. One can always tell from a woman's bonnet whether she has got a memory or not.

There are things that are right to say but that may be said at the wrong time and to the wrong people.

The meaning of any beautiful created thing is, at least, as much in the soul of him who looks at it as it was in his soul who wrought it. Nay, it is rather the beholder who lends to the beautiful thing its myriad meanings, and makes it marvellous for us, and sets it in some new relation to the age, so that it becomes a vital portion of our lives and a symbol of what we pray for, or perhaps of what, having prayed for, we fear that we may receive.

The Renaissance was great because it sought to solve no social problem, and busied itself not about such things, but suffered the individual to develop freely, beautifully, and naturally, and so had great and individual artists and great and individual men.

In England people actually try to be brilliant at breakfast. That is so dreadful of them! Only dull people are brilliant at breakfast.

When one is in love one begins by deceiving oneself, and one ends by deceiving others. That is what the world calls a romance.

The secret of life is never to have an emotion that is unbecoming.

No artist is ever morbid. The artist can express everything.

The development of the race depends on the development of the individual, and where self-culture has ceased to be the ideal the intellectual standard is instantly lowered and often ultimately lost.

An idea that is not dangerous is unworthy of being called an idea at all.

To elope is cowardly; it is running away from danger, and danger has become so rare in modern life.

When a man is old enough to do wrong he should be old enough to do right also.

The Book of Life begins with a man and a woman in a garden. It ends with Revelations.

In married life three is company and two is none.

Out of ourselves we can never pass, nor can there be in creation what in the creator was not.

Don't tell me that you have exhausted life. When a man says that one knows that life has exhausted him.

When a woman marries again it is because she detested her first husband. When a man marries again it is because he adored his first wife. Women try their luck; men risk theirs.

The highest criticism really is the record of one's own soul. It is more fascinating than history, as it is concerned simply with oneself. It is more delightful than philosophy, as its subject is concrete and not abstract, real and not vague. It is the only civilised form of autobiography, as it deals, not with the events, but with the thoughts of one's life, not with life's physical accidents of deed or circumstance, but with the spiritual moods and imaginative passions of the mind.

To know anything about oneself one must know all about others.

Duty is what one expects from others, it is not what one does oneself.

After a good dinner one can forgive anybody, even one's own relations.

Talk to every woman as if you loved her and to every man as if he bored you, and at the end of your first season you will have the reputation of possessing the most perfect social tact.

Man—poor, awkward, reliable, necessary man—belongs to a sex that has been rational for millions and millions of years. He can't help himself; it is in his race. The history of women is very different. They have always been picturesque protests against the mere existence of common-sense; they saw its dangers from the first.

More marriages are ruined nowadays by the common-sense of the husband than by anything else. How can a woman be expected to be happy with a man who insists on treating her as if she were a perfectly rational being.

It is very vulgar to talk about one's business. Only people like stock-brokers do that, and then merely at dinner-parties.

It is awfully hard work doing nothing. However, I don't mind hard work when there is no definite object of any kind.

To do nothing at all is the most difficult thing in the world, the most difficult and the most intellectual. To Plato, with his passion for wisdom, this was the noblest form of energy.

To Aristotle, with his passion for knowledge, this was the noblest form of energy also. It was to this that the passion for holiness led the saint and the mystic of mediæval days.

Youth! There is nothing like it. It is absurd to talk of the ignorance of youth. The only people to whose opinions I listen now with any respect are persons much younger than myself. They seem in front of me. Life has revealed to them her latest wonder.

Romance lives by repetition, and repetition converts an appetite into an art.

I adore simple pleasures. They are the last refuge of the complex.

There is nothing like youth. The middle-aged are mortgaged to life. The old are in life's lumber-room. But youth is the lord of life. Youth has a kingdom waiting for it. Everyone is born a king, and most people die in exile—like most kings.

All crime is vulgar, just as all vulgarity is crime.

Society, civilised society at least, is never very ready to believe anything to the detriment of those who are both rich and fascinating. It instinctively feels that manners are of more importance than morals, and in its opinion the highest respectability is of much less value than the possession of a good chef. And, after all, it is a very poor consolation to be told that the man who has given one a bad dinner or poor wine is irreproachable in his private life. Even the cardinal virtues cannot atone for half-cold entrees.

While, in the opinion of society, contemplation is the gravest thing of which any citizen can be guilty, in the opinion of the highest culture it is the proper occupation of man.

Life is terribly deficient in form. Its catastrophes happen in the wrong way and to the wrong people. There is a grotesque horror about its comedies, and its tragedies seem to culminate in farce. One is always wounded when one approaches it. Things last either too long or not long enough.

If a woman wants to hold a man she has merely to appeal to what is worst in him.

We are all in the gutter, but some of us are looking at the stars.

Beauty has as many meanings as man has moods. It is the symbol of symbols. It reveals everything, because it expresses nothing. When it shows us itself it shows us the whole fiery-coloured world.

Men always want to be a woman's first love. That is their clumsy vanity. Women have a more subtle instinct about things. What they like is to be a man's last romance.

Anything approaching to the free play of the mind is practically unknown amongst us. People cry out against the sinner, yet it is not the sinful but the stupid who are our shame. There is no sin except stupidity.

One regrets the loss even of one's worst habits. Perhaps one regrets them the most. They are such an essential part of one's personality.

It is through art, and through art only, that we can realise our perfection; through art and through art only, that we can shield ourselves from the sordid perils of actual existence.

A man who can dominate a London dinner-table can dominate the world. The future belongs to the dandy. It is the exquisites who are going to rule.

It often happens that the real tragedies of life occur in such an inartistic manner that they hurt us by their crude violence, their absolute incoherence, their absurd want of meaning, their entire lack of style. They affect us just as vulgarity affects us. They give us an impression of sheer brute force, and we revolt against that. Sometimes, however, a tragedy that possesses artistic elements of beauty crosses our lives. If these elements of beauty are real the whole thing simply appeals to our sense of dramatic effect. Suddenly we find that we are no longer the actors but the spectators of the play. Or rather we are both. We watch ourselves, and the mere wonder of the spectacle enthrals us.

When a woman finds out that her husband is absolutely indifferent to her, she either becomes dreadfully dowdy or wears very smart bonnets that some other woman's husband has to pay for.

It is immoral to use private property in order to alleviate the horrible evils that result from the institution of private property.

It is a mistake to think that the passion one feels in creation is ever really shown in the work one creates. Art is always more abstract than we fancy. Form and colour tell us of form and colour-that is all.

It is sometimes said that the tragedy of an artist's life is that he cannot realise his ideal. But the true tragedy that dogs the steps of most artists is that they realise their ideal too absolutely. For when the ideal is realised it is robbed of its wonder and its mystery, and becomes simply a new starting-point for an ideal that is other than itself.

People who go in for being consistent have just as many moods as others have. The only difference is that their moods are rather meaningless.

It is only shallow people who require years to get rid of an emotion. A man who is master of himself can end a sorrow as easily as he can invent a pleasure.

Good women have such a limited view of life, their horizon is so small, their interests so petty. The fact is they are not modern, and to be modern is the only thing worth being nowadays.

Discontent is the first step in the progress of a man or a nation.

Men marry because they are tired, women because they are curious. Both are disappointed.

All men are married women's property. That is the only true definition of what married women's property really is.

I am not in favour of this modern mania for turning bad people into good people at a moment's notice. As a man sows so let him reap.

Nothing refines but the intellect.

It is very painful for me to be forced to speak the truth. It is the first time in my life that I have ever been reduced to such a painful position, and I am really quite inexperienced in doing anything of the kind.

The man who regards his past is a man who deserves to have no future to look forward to.

Just as it is only by contact with the art of foreign nations that the art of a country gains that individual and separate life that we call nationality, so, by curious inversion, it is only by intensifying his own personality that the critic can interpret the personality of others; and the more strongly this personality enters into the interpretation the more real the interpretation becomes, the more satisfying, the more convincing, and the more true.

Man is least himself when he talks in his own person. Give him a mask, and he will tell you the truth.

All women become like their mothers: that is their tragedy. No man does: that is his.

Women are a fascinatingly wilful sex. Every woman is a rebel, and usually in wild revolt against herself.

One should always be in love. That is the reason one should never marry.

No man came across two ideal things. Few come across one.

To become the spectator of one's own life is to escape the suffering of life.

The state is to make what is useful. The individual is to make what is beautiful.

A community is infinitely more brutalised by the habitual employment of punishment than it is by the occasional occurrence of crime.

The systems that fail are those that rely on the permanency of human nature and not on its growth and development.

Jealousy, which is an extraordinary source of crime in modern life, is an emotion closely bound up with our conceptions of property, and under socialism and individualism will die out. It is remarkable that in communistic tribes jealousy is entirely unknown.

All art is immoral.

He to whom the present is the only thing that is present knows nothing of the age in which he lives. To realise the nineteenth century one must realise every century that has preceded it and that has contributed to its making.

Few parents nowadays pay any regard to what their children say to them. The old-fashioned respect for the young is fast dying out.

The history of woman is the history of the worst form of tyranny the world has ever known; the tyranny of the weak over the strong. It is the only tyranny that lasts.

The happiness of a married man depends on the people he has not married.

There is no one type for man. There are as many perfections as there are imperfect men. And while to the claims of charity a man may yield and yet be free, to the claims of conformity no man may yield and remain free at all.

A practical scheme is either a scheme that is already in existence or a scheme that could be carried out under existing conditions.

All imitation in morals and in life is wrong.

The world has been made by fools that wise men may live in it.

Women love us for our defects. If we have enough of them they will forgive us everything, even our gigantic intellects.

Society is a necessary thing. No man has any real success in this world unless he has got women to back him—and women rule society. If you have not got women on your side you are quite over. You might just as well be a barrister or a stockbroker or a journalist at once.

The worship of the senses has often, and with much justice, been decried; men feeling a natural instinct of terror about passions and sensations that seem stronger than themselves, and that they are conscious of sharing with the less highly organised forms of existence. But it is probable the true nature of the senses has never been understood, and that they have remained savage and animal merely because the world has sought to starve them into submission or to kill them by pain instead of aiming at making them elements of a new spirituality, of which a fine instinct for beauty will be the dominant characteristic.

Women appreciate cruelty more than anything else. They have wonderfully primitive instincts. We have emancipated them, but they remain slaves, looking for their master all the same. They love being dominated.

Those who try to lead the people can only do so by following the mob. It is through the voice of one crying in the wilderness that the way of the gods must be prepared.

Circumstances are the lashes laid on to us by life. Some of us have to receive them with bared ivory backs, and others are permitted to keep on a coat—that is the only difference.

Criticism is itself an art.... It is no more to be judged by any low standard of imitation or resemblance than is the work of poet or sculptor. The critic occupies the same relation to the work of art that he criticises as the artist does to the visible world of form and colour or the unseen world of passion and thought. He does not even require for the perfection of his art the finest materials. Anything will serve his purpose.

It is very much more difficult to talk about a thing than to do it. In the sphere of actual life that is, of course, obvious. Anybody can make history, only a great man can write it.

If we lived long enough to see the results of our actions it may be that those who call themselves good would be filled with a wild remorse and those whom the world calls evil stirred with a noble joy. Each little thing that we do passes into the great machine of life, which may grind our virtues to powder and make them worthless or transform our sins into elements of a new civilisation more marvellous and more splendid than any that has gone before.

Children begin by loving their parents; as they grow older they judge them, sometimes they forgive them.

We live in an age that reads too much to be wise and that thinks too much to be beautiful.

One should absorb the colour of life, but one should never remember its details. Details are always vulgar.

It will be a marvellous thing—the true personality of man—when we see it. It will grow naturally and simply flowerlike, or as a tree grows. It will not be at discord. It will never argue or dispute. It will not prove things. It will know everything, and yet it will not busy itself about knowledge. It will have wisdom. Its value will not be measured by material things. It will have nothing, and yet it will have everything, and whatever one takes from it it will still have, so rich it will be. It will not be always meddling with others or asking them to be like itself. It will love them because they will be different. And yet, while it will not meddle with others, it will help all, as a beautiful thing helps us, by being what it is. The personality of man will be very wonderful. It will be as wonderful as the personality of a child.

Cynicism is merely the art of seeing things as they are instead of as they ought to be.

Three addresses always inspire confidence, even in tradesmen.

If one doesn't talk about a thing it has never happened. It is simply expression that gives reality to things.

No man is able who is unable to get on, just as no woman is clever who can't succeed in obtaining that worst and most necessary of evils, a husband.

The one charm of the past is that it is the past. But women never know when the curtain has fallen. They always want a sixth act, and as soon as the interest of the play is entirely over they propose to continue it. If they were allowed their way every comedy would have a tragic ending and every tragedy would culminate in a farce. They are charmingly artificial, but they have no sense of art.

Each time that one loves is the only time that one has ever loved. Difference of object does not alter singleness of passion. It merely intensifies it.

The real tragedy of the poor is that they can afford nothing but self-denial. Beautiful sins, like beautiful things, are the privilege of the rich.

Human life is the one thing worth investigating. Compared to it there is nothing else of any value. It is true that as one watches life in its curious crucible of pain and pleasure one cannot wear over one's face a mask of glass nor keep the sulphurous fumes from troubling the brain and making the imagination turbid with monstrous fancies and misshapen dreams. There are poisons so subtle that to know their properties one has to sicken of them. There are maladies so strange that one has to pass through them if one seeks to understand their nature. And yet what a great reward one receives! How wonderful the whole world becomes to one! To note the curious, hard logic of passion and the emotional, coloured life of the intellect—to observe where they meet, and where they separate, at what point they are in unison and at what point they are in discord—there is a delight in that! What matter what the cost is? One can never pay too high a price for any sensation.

There is only one class in the community that thinks more about money than the rich, and that is the poor. The poor can think of nothing else. That is the misery of being poor.

To live is the rarest thing in the world. Most people exist—that is all.

Personality is a very mysterious thing. A man cannot always be estimated by what he does. He may keep the law, and yet be worthless. He may break the law, and yet be fine. He may be bad without ever doing anything bad. He may commit a sin against society, and yet realise through that sin his true perfection.

Mediæval art is charming, but mediæval emotions are out of date. One can use them in fiction, of course; but then the only things that one can use in fiction are the only things that one has ceased to use in fact.

Man is complete in himself.

What is a cynic? A man who knows the price of everything and the value of nothing.

It's the old, old story. Love—well, not at first sight—but love at the end

40

of the season, which is so much more satisfactory.

No nice girl should ever waltz with such particularly younger sons! It looks so fast!

Good resolutions are useless attempts to interfere with scientific laws. Their origin is pure vanity. Their result is absolutely nil. They give us now and then some of those luxurious, sterile emotions that have a certain charm for the weak. That is all that can be said for them. They are simply cheques that men draw on a bank where they have no account.

What is the difference between literature and journalism? Journalism is unreadable and literature is unread.

I hope you have not been leading a double life, pretending to be wicked and being really good all the time. That would be hypocrisy.

My husband is a sort of promissory note; I am tired of meeting him.

Conscience makes egotists of us all.

Never trust a woman who wears mauve, whatever her age may be, or a woman over thirty-five who is fond of pink ribbons. It always means that they have a history.

There is a fatality about good resolutions-they are always made too late.

We can have in life but one great experience at best, and the secret of life is to reproduce that experience as often as possible.

Anybody can be good in the country. There are no temptations there. That is the reason why people who live out of town are so absolutely uncivilised. Civilisation is not by any means an easy thing to attain to. There are only two ways by which man can reach it. One is by being cultured, the other by being corrupt. Country people have no opportunity of being either, so they stagnate.

What nonsense people talk about happy marriages! A man can be happy with any woman so long as he does not love her.

The things one feels absolutely certain about are never true. That is the fatality of faith and the lesson of romance.

In the common world of fact the wicked are not punished nor the good rewarded. Success is given to the strong, failure thrust upon the weak.

Nothing should be able to harm a man except himself. Nothing should be able to rob a man at all. What a man really has is what is in him. What is outside of him should be a matter of no importance.

Modern morality consists in accepting the standard of one's age. I consider that for any man of culture to accept the standard of his age is a form of the grossest immorality.

Perplexity and mistrust fan affection into passion, and so bring about those beautiful tragedies that alone make life worth living. Women once felt this, while men did not, and so women once ruled the world.

Sin is a thing that writes itself across a man's, face. It cannot be concealed. People talk sometimes of secret vices. There are no such things.

If a wretched man has a vice it shows itself in the lines of his mouth, the drop of his eyelids, the moulding of his hands even.

There are sins whose fascination is more in the memory than in the doing of them, strange triumphs that gratify the pride more than the passions and give to the intellect a quickened sense of joy, greater than they bring or can ever bring to the senses.

No civilised man ever regrets a pleasure, and no uncivilised man ever knows what a pleasure is.

As for a spoiled life, no life is spoiled but one whose growth is arrested. If you want to mar a nature you have merely to reform it.

Socialism itself will be of value simply because it will lead to individualism.

Some years ago people went about the country saying that property has duties. It is perfectly true. Property not merely has duties, but has so many duties that its possession to any large extent is a bore. If property had simply pleasures we could stand it, but its duties make it unbearable.

It is through joy that the individualism of the future will develop itself. Christ made no attempt to reconstruct society, and consequently the individualism that He preached to man could be realised only through pain or in solitude.

Most people become bankrupt through having invested too heavily in the prose of life. To have ruined oneself over poetry is an honour.

The only artists I have ever known who are personally delightful are bad artists. Good artists exist simply on what they make, and consequently are perfectly uninteresting in what they are.

What are the virtues? Nature, Renan tells us, cares little about chastity, and it may be that it is to the shame of the Magdalen, and not to their own purity, that the Lucretias of modern life owe their freedom from stain. Charity, as even those of whose religion it makes a formal part have been compelled to acknowledge, creates a multitude of evils. The mere existence of conscience, that faculty of which people prate so much nowadays, and are so ignorantly proud, is a sign of our imperfect development. It must be merged in instinct before we become fine. Self-denial is simply a method by which man arrests his progress, and self-sacrifice a survival of the mutilation of the savage, part of that old worship of pain which is so terrible a factor in the history of the world, and which even now makes its victims day by day and has its altars in the land. Virtues! Who knows what the virtues are? Not you. Not I. Not anyone. It is well for our vanity that we slay the criminal, for if we suffered him to live he might show us what we had gained by his crime. It is well for his peace that the saint goes to his martyrdom. He is spared the sight of the horror of his harvest.

Nowadays all the married men live like bachelors and all the bachelors like married men.

The higher education of men is what I should like to see. Men need it so sadly.

The world is perfectly packed with good women. To know them is a middle-class education.

Hesitation of any kind is a sign of mental decay in the young, of physical weakness in the old.

Our husbands never appreciate anything in us. We have to go to others for that.

Most women in London nowadays seem to furnish their rooms with nothing but orchids, foreigners and French novels.

The canons of good society are, or should be, the same as the canons of art. Form is absolutely essential to it. It should have the dignity of a ceremony as well as its unreality, and should combine the insincere character of a romantic play with the wit and beauty that make such plays delightful to us. Is sincerity such a terrible thing? I think not. It is merely a method by which we can multiply our personalities.

The tragedy of old age is not that one is old but that one is young.

A great poet, a really great poet, is the most unpoetical of all creatures. But inferior poets are absolutely fascinating. The worse their rhymes are the more picturesque they look. The mere fact of having published a book of second-rate sonnets makes a man quite irresistible. He lives the poetry that he cannot write. The others write the poetry that they dare not realise.

Being adored is a nuisance. Women treat us just as humanity treats its gods. They worship us, and are always bothering us to do something for them.

If a man treats life artistically his brain is his heart.

The 'Peerage' is the one book a young man about town should know thoroughly, and it is the best thing in fiction the English have ever done.

The world has always laughed at its own tragedies, that being the only way in which it has been able to bear them. Consequently whatever the world has treated seriously belongs to the comedy side of things.

The only difference between the saint and the sinner is that every saint has a past and every sinner has a future.

What is termed sin is an essential element of progress. Without it the world would stagnate or grow old or becomes colourless. By its curiosity it increases the experience of the race. Through its intensified assertion of individualism it saves us from the commonplace. In its rejection of the current notions about morality it is one with the higher ethics.

Formerly we used to canonise our heroes. The modern method is to vulgarise them. Cheap editions of great books may be delightful, but cheap editions of great men are absolutely detestable.

Individualism does not come to man with any claims upon him at all. It comes naturally and inevitably out of man. It is the point to which all development tends. It is the differentiation to which all organisms grow. It is the perfection that is inherent in every mode of life and toward which every mode of life quickens. Individualism exercises no compulsion over man. On the contrary, it says to man that he should suffer no compulsion to be exercised over him. It does not try to force people to be good. It knows that people are good when they are let alone. Man will develop individualism out of himself. Man is now so developing individualism. To ask whether individualism is practical is like asking whether evolution is practical. Evolution is the law of life, and there is no evolution except towards individualism.

The longer I live the more keenly I feel that whatever was good enough for our fathers is not good enough for us. In art, as in politics, 'les grand pères ont toujours tort.'

No woman is a genius. Women are a decorative sex. They never have anything to say but they say it charmingly.

Humanity takes itself too seriously. It is the world's original sin. If the cave men had known how to laugh history would have been different.

I wonder who it was defined man as a rational animal. It was the most premature definition ever given. Man is many things, but he is not rational.

Thought and language are to the artist instruments of an art.

To get into the best society nowadays one has either to feed people, amuse people, or shock people—that is all.

You should never try to understand women. Women are pictures, men are problems. If you want to know what a woman really means—which, by the way, is always a dangerous thing to do—look at her, don't listen to her.

Ordinary women never appeal to one's imagination. They are limited to their century. No glamour ever transfigures them. One knows their minds as easily as one knows their bonnets. One can always find them. There is no mystery in any of them. They ride in the park in the morning and chatter at tea parties in the afternoon. They have their stereotyped smile and their fashionable mauve.

Don't run down dyed hair and painted faces. There is an extraordinary charm in them—sometimes.

To have been well brought up is a great drawback nowadays. It shuts one out from so much.

The people who have adored me—there have not been very many, but there have been some—have always insisted on living on long after I had ceased to care for them or they to care for me. They have become stout and tedious, and when I meet them they go in at once for reminiscences. That awful memory of women! What a fearful thing it is! And what an utter intellectual stagnation it reveals!

Examinations are pure humbug from beginning to end. If a man is a gentleman he knows quite enough, and if he is not a gentleman whatever he knows is bad for him.

Credit is the capital of a younger son, and he can live charmingly on it.

The object of art is not simply truth but complex beauty. Art itself is really a form of exaggeration, and selection, which is the very spirit of art, is nothing more than an intensified mode of over-emphasis.

The popular cry of our time is: 'Let us return to Life and Nature, they will recreate Art for us and send the red blood coursing through her veins; they will shoe her feet with swiftness and make her hand strong.' But, alas! we are mistaken in our amiable and well-meant efforts. Nature is always behind the age. And as for life, she is the solvent that breaks up Art, the enemy that lays waste her house.

There are only two kinds of women—the plain and the coloured. The plain women are very useful. If you want to gain a reputation for respectability you have merely to take them down to supper. The other women are very charming. They commit one mistake, however—they paint in order to try and look young.

The way of paradoxes is the way of truth. To test reality we must see it on the tight-rope. When the verities become acrobats we can judge them.

Life imitates art far more than art imitates life.... The Greeks with their quick, artistic instinct understood this, and set in the bride's chamber the statue of Hermes or of Apollo, that she might bear children as lovely as the works of art that she looked at in her rapture or her pain. They knew that life gains from art not merely spirituality, depth of thought and feeling, soul-turmoil or soul-peace, but that she can form herself on the very lines and colours of art, and can reproduce the dignity of Pheidias as well as the grace of Praxiteles. Hence came this objection to realism. They disliked it on purely social grounds. They felt that it inevitably makes people ugly, and they were perfectly right.

Faithfulness is to the emotional life what consistency is to the life of the intellect—simply a confession of failure.

There are many things that we would throw away if we were not afraid that others might pick them up.

What a fuss people make about fidelity! Why, even in love it is purely a question for physiology. It has nothing to do with our own will. Young men want to be faithful and are not; old men want to be faithless and cannot—that is all one can say.

Modernity of form and modernity of subject-matter are entirely and absolutely wrong. We have mistaken the common livery of the age for the vesture of the muses, and spent our days in the sordid streets and hideous suburbs of our vile cities when we should be out on the hillside with Apollo.

Certainly we are a degraded race, and have sold our birthright for a mess of facts.

Nothing can cure the soul but the senses, just as nothing can cure the senses but the soul.

I can stand brute force, but brute reason is quite unbearable. There is something unfair about its use. It is hitting below the intellect.

Those who live in marble or on painted panel know of life but a single exquisite instant, eternal, indeed, in its beauty but limited to one note of passion or one mood of calm. Those whom the poet makes live have their myriad emotions of joy and terror, of courage and despair, of pleasure and of suffering. The seasons come and go in glad or saddening pageant, and with winged or leaden feet the years pass by before them. They have their youth and their manhood, they are children, and they grow old. It is always dawn for St Helena as Veronese saw her at the window. Through the still morning air the angels bring her the symbol of God's pain. The cool breezes of the morning lift the gilt threads from her brow. On that little hill by the city of Florence, where the lovers of Giorgione are lying, it is always the solstice of noon—of noon made so languorous by summer suns that hardly can the slim, naked girl dip into the marble tank the round bubble of clear glass, and the long fingers of the lute player rest idly upon the chords. It is twilight always for the dancing nymphs whom Corot set free among the silver poplars of France. In eternal twilight they move, those frail, diaphanous figures, whose tremulous, white feet seem not to touch the dew-drenched grass they tread on. But those who walk in epos, drama, or romance see through the labouring months the young moons wax and wane, and watch the night from evening into morning star, and from sunrise into sun-setting can note the shifting day with all its gold and shadow. For them, as for us, the flowers bloom and wither, and the earth, that green-tressed goddess, as Coleridge calls her, alters her raiment for their pleasure. The statue is concentrated to one moment of perfection. The image stained upon the canvas possesses no spiritual element of growth or change. If they know nothing of death it is because they know little of life, for the secrets of life and death belong to those, and to those only, whom the sequence of time affects, and who possess not merely the present but the future, and can rise or fall from a past of glory or of shame. Movement, that problem of the visible arts, can be truly realised by literature alone. It is literature that shows us the body in its swiftness and the soul in its unrest.

Behind every exquisite thing that exists there is something tragic. Worlds have to be in travail that the merest flower may blow.

Beauty is a form of genius—is higher, indeed, than genius, as it needs no explanation. It is one of the great facts of the world, like sunlight, or spring-time, or the reflection in dark water of that silver shell we call the moon. It cannot be questioned, it has its divine right of sovereignty.

The only way to get rid of a temptation is to yield to it. Resist it and your soul grows sick with longing for the things it has forbidden to itself.

Women spoil every romance by trying to make it last for ever.

He's sure to be a wonderful success. He thinks like a Tory and talks like a Radical, and that's so important nowadays.

Nowadays to be intelligible is to be found out.

We make gods of men and they leave us. Others make brutes of them and they fawn and are faithful.

The husbands of very beautiful women belong to the criminal classes.

To me beauty is the Wonder of wonders. It is only shallow people who do not judge by appearances.

The true mystery of the world is the visible, not the invisible.

The thoroughly well-informed man is the modern ideal. And the mind of the thoroughly well-informed man is a dreadful thing. It is like a bric-a-brac shop, all monsters and dust, with everything priced above its proper value.

Women have no appreciation of good looks in men—at least good women have none.

To influence a person is to give him one's own soul. He does not think his natural thoughts or burn with his natural passions. His virtues are not real to him. His sins, if there are such things as sins, are borrowed. He becomes an echo of someone else's music, an actor of a part that has not been written for him.

Those who are faithful know only the trivial side of love; it is the faithless who know love's tragedies.

An artist should create beautiful things, but should put nothing of his own life into them. We live in an age when men treat art as if it were meant to be a form of autobiography. We have lost the abstract sense of beauty.

A man cannot be too careful in the choice of his enemies. I have not got one who is a fool. They are all men of some intellectual power, and consequently they all appreciate me.

The value of an idea has nothing whatever to do with the sincerity of the man who expresses it.

I like persons better than principles, and I like persons with no principles better than anything else in the world.

He who would lead a Christ-like life is he who is perfectly and absolutely himself. He may be a great poet, or a great man of science; or a young student at the university, or one who watches sheep upon a moor; or a maker of dramas, like Shakespeare, or a thinker about God, like Spinoza; or a child who plays in a garden, or a fisherman who throws his nets into the sea. It does not matter what he is as long as he realises the perfection of the soul that is within him.

The aim of life is self-development. To realise one's nature perfectly—that is what each of us is here for.

There is no such thing as a good influence. All influence is immoral—immoral from the scientific point of view.

Words have not merely music as sweet as that of viol and lute, colour as rich and vivid as any that makes lovely for us the canvas of the Venetian or the Spaniard, and plastic form no less sure and certain than that which reveals itself in marble or in bronze, but thought and passion and spirituality are theirs also—are theirs, indeed, alone.

There is nothing so absolutely pathetic as a really fine paradox. The pun is the clown among jokes, the well-turned paradox is the polished comedian, and the highest comedy verges upon tragedy, just as the keenest edge of tragedy is often tempered by a subtle humour. Our minds are shot with moods as a fabric is shot with colours, and our moods often seem inappropriate. Everything that is true is inappropriate.

The longer one studies life and literature the more strongly one feels that behind everything that is wonderful stands the individual, and that it is not the moment that makes the man but the man who creates the age.

To know the vintage and quality of a wine one need not drink the whole cask.

It is a sad thing to think of, but there is no doubt that genius lasts longer than beauty. That accounts for the fact that we all take such pains to over-educate ourselves.

The ugly and the stupid have the best of it in this world. They can sit at their ease and gape at the play. If they know nothing of victory they are at least spared the knowledge of defeat.

To have a capacity for a passion, and not to realise it is to make oneself incomplete and limited.

Even in actual life egotism is not without its attractions. When people talk to us about others they are usually dull. When they talk to us about themselves they are nearly always interesting, and if one could shut them up when they become wearisome as easily as one can shut up a book of which one has grown wearied they would be perfect absolutely.

Every great man nowadays has his disciples and it is invariably Judas who writes the biography.

Art finds her own perfection within, and not outside of, herself. She is not to be judged by any external standard of resemblance. She is a veil rather than a mirror. She has flowers that no forest knows of, birds that no woodland possesses. She makes and unmakes many worlds, and can draw the moon from heaven with a scarlet thread. Hers are the 'forms more real than living man,' and hers the great archetypes, of which things that have existence are but unfinished copies. Nature has, in her eyes, no laws, no uniformity. She can work miracles at her will, and when she calls monsters from the deep they come. She can bid the almond-tree blossom in winter and send the snow upon the ripe cornfield. At her word the frost lays its silver finger on the burning mouth of June, and the winged lions creep out from the hollows of the Lydian hills. The dryads peer from the thicket as she passes by, and the brown fauns smile strangely at her when she comes near them. She has hawk-faced gods that worship her, and the centaurs gallop at her side.

In literature mere egotism is delightful.

If we live for aims we blunt our emotions. If we live for aims we live for one minute, for one day, for one year, instead of for every minute, every day, every year. The moods of one's life are life's beauties. To yield to all one's moods is to really live.

Many a young man starts in life with a natural gift for exaggeration which, if nurtured in congenial and sympathetic surroundings, or by the imitations of the best models, might grow into something really great and wonderful. But, as a rule, he comes to nothing. He either falls into careless habits of accuracy or takes to frequenting the society of the aged and the well-informed. Both things are equally fatal to his imagination.

The spirit of an age may be best expressed in the abstract ideal arts, for the spirit itself is abstract and ideal.

As for believing things, I can believe anything provided that it is quite incredible.

'Know thyself' was written over the portal of the antique world. Over the portal of the new world 'Be thyself' shall be written. And the message of Christ to man was simply: 'Be thyself.' That is the secret of Christ.

London is full of women who trust their husbands. One can always recognise them, they look so thoroughly unhappy.

For those who are not artists, and to whom there is no mode of life but the actual life of fact, pain is the only door to perfection.

The English public always feels perfectly at its ease when a mediocrity is talking to it.

Men always fall into the absurdity of endeavouring to develop the mind, to push it violently forward in this direction or in that. The mind should be receptive, a harp waiting to catch the winds, a pool ready to be ruffled, not a bustling busybody for ever trotting about on the pavement looking for a new bun shop.

There is nothing more beautiful than to forget, except, perhaps, to be forgotten.

All bad art comes from returning to life and nature, and elevating them into ideals. Life and nature may sometimes be used as part of art's rough material, but before they are of any real service to art they must be translated into artistic conventions. The moment art surrenders its imaginative medium it surrenders everything. As a method realism is a complete failure, and the two things that every artist should avoid are modernity of form and modernity of subject-matter.

Men may have women's minds just as women may have the minds of men.

London is too full of fogs and serious people. Whether the fogs produce the serious people or whether the serious people produce the fogs I don't know.

How marriage ruins a man! It's as demoralising as cigarettes, and far more expensive.

He must be quite respectable. One has never heard his name before in the whole course of one's life, which speaks volumes for a man nowadays.

Literature always anticipates life. It does not copy it, but moulds it to its purpose.

As long as a thing is useful or necessary to us or affects us in any way, either for pain or pleasure, or appeals strongly to our sympathies or is a vital part of the environment in which we live, it is outside the proper sphere of art.

I couldn't have a scene in this bonnet: it is far too fragile. A harsh word would ruin it.

Music creates for one a past of which one has been ignorant and fills one with a sense of sorrows that have been hidden from one's tears.

Nothing is so fatal to personality as deliberation.

I adore London dinner parties. The clever people never listen and the stupid people never talk.

Learned conversation is either the affection of the ignorant or the profession of the mentally unemployed.

The Academy is too large and too vulgar. Whenever I have gone there, there have been either so many people that I have not been able to see the pictures—which was dreadful, or so many pictures that I have not been able to see the people—which was worse.

All art is quite useless.

Beauty, real beauty, ends where an intellectual expression begins. Intellect is in itself a mode of exaggeration and destroys the harmony of any face. The moment one sits down to think one becomes all nose or all forehead or something horrid.

The one charm of marriage is that it makes a life of deception absolutely necessary for both parties.

Secrecy seems to be the one thing that can make modern life mysterious or marvellous to us. The commonest thing is delightful if one only hides it.

Conceit is one of the greatest of the virtues, yet how few people recognise it as a thing to aim at and to strive after. In conceit many a man and woman has found salvation, yet the average person goes on all-fours grovelling after modesty.

It is difficult not to be unjust to what one loves.

Humanity will always love Rousseau for having confessed his sins not to a friend but to the world.

Just as those who do not love Plato more than truth cannot pass beyond the threshold of the Academe, so those who do not love beauty more than truth never know the inmost shrine of art.

There is a fatality about all physical and intellectual distinction: the sort of fatality that seems to dog, through history, the faltering steps of kings. It is better not to be different from one's fellows.

To be born, or at any rate bred, in a handbag, whether it had handles or not, seems to me to display a contempt for the ordinary decencies of family life that reminds one of the worst excesses of the French Revolution.

Vice and virtue are to the artist materials for an art.

There must be a new Hedonism that shall recreate life and save it from that harsh, uncomely Puritanism that is having, in our own day, its curious revival. It must have its service of the intellect, certainly, yet it must never accept any theory or system that will involve the sacrifice of any mode of passionate experience. Its aim, indeed, is to be experience itself and not the fruits of experience, bitter or sweet as they may be. Of the æstheticism that deadens the senses, as of the vulgar profligacy that dulls them, it is to know nothing. But it is to teach man to concentrate himself upon the moments of a life that is itself but a moment.

Art never expresses anything but itself. It has an independent life, just as thought has, and develops purely on its own lines. It is not necessarily realistic in an age of realism nor spiritual in an age of faith. So far from being the creation of its time it is usually in direct opposition to it, and the only history that it preserves for us is the history of its own progress.

People who mean well always do badly. They are like the ladies who wear clothes that don't fit them in order to show their piety. Good intentions are invariably ungrammatical.

Man can believe the impossible, but man can never believe the improbable.

When art is more varied nature will, no doubt, be more varied also.

If a man is sufficiently imaginative to produce evidence in support of a lie he might just as well speak the truth at once.

The ancient historians gave us delightful fiction in the form of fact; the modern novelist presents us with dull facts under the guise of fiction.

Nature is no great mother who has home us. She is our own creation. It is in our brain that she quickens to life. Things are because we see them, and what we see and how we see it depends on the arts that have influenced us. To look at a thing is very different from seeing a thing. One does not see anything until one sees its beauty.

The proper school to learn art in is not life but art.

I won't tell you that the world matters nothing, or the world's voice, or the voice of society. They matter a good deal. They matter far too much.

I wouldn't marry a man with a future before him for anything under the sun.

I am the only person in the world I should like to know thoroughly, but I don't see any chance of it just at present.

Modern memoirs are generally written by people who have entirely lost their memories and have never done anything worth recording.

Education is an admirable thing, but it is well to remember from time to time that nothing that is worth knowing can be taught.

Women are like minors, they live upon their expectations.

Twisted minds are as natural to some people as twisted bodies.

It is the very passions about whose origin we deceive ourselves that tyrannise most strongly over us. Our weakest motives are those of whose nature we are conscious. It often happens that when we think we are experimenting on others we are really experimenting on ourselves.

Whenever a man does a thoroughly stupid thing it is always from the noblest motives.

I thought I had no heart. I find I have, and a heart doesn't suit me. Somehow it doesn't go with modern dress. It makes one look old, and it spoils one's career at critical moments.

I don't play accurately—anyone can play accurately—but I play with wonderful expression. As far as the piano is concerned sentiment is my forte. I keep science for life.

I delight in men over seventy. They always offer one the devotion of a lifetime.

Everybody who is incapable of learning has taken to teaching—that is really what our enthusiasm for education has come to.

Nature hates mind.

From the point of view of form the type of all the arts is the art of the musician. From the point of view of feeling the actor's craft is the type.

Where we differ from each other is purely in accidentals—in dress, manner, tone of voice, religious opinions, personal appearance, tricks of habit, and the like.

The more we study art the less we care for Nature. What art really reveals to us is Nature's lack of design, her curious crudities, her extraordinary monotony, her absolutely unfinished condition.... It is fortunate for us, however, that nature is so imperfect, as otherwise we should have had no art at all. Art is our spirited protest, our gallant attempt to teach Nature her proper place. As for the infinite variety of nature, that is a pure myth. It is not to be found in Nature herself. It resides in the imagination or fancy or cultivated blindness of the man who looks at her.

Facts are not merely finding a footing-place in history but they are usurping the domain of fancy and have invaded the kingdom of romance. Their chilling touch is over everything. They are vulgarising mankind.

Ordinary people wait till life discloses to them its secrets, but to the few, to the elect, the mysteries of life are revealed before the veil is drawn away. Sometimes this is the effect of art, and chiefly of the art of literature which deals immediately with the passions and the intellect. But now and then a complex personality takes the place and assumes the office of art, is, indeed, in its way a real work of art, Life having its elaborate masterpieces just as poetry has, or sculpture, or painting.

Thinking is the most unhealthy thing in the world, and people die of it just as they die of any other disease.

A cigarette is the perfect type of a perfect pleasure. It is exquisite and it leaves one unsatisfied.

The aim of the liar is simply to charm, to delight, to give pleasure. He is the very basis of civilised society.

It is quite a mistake to believe, as many people do, that the mind shows itself in the face. Vice may sometimes write itself in lines and changes of contour, but that is all. Our faces are really masks given to us to conceal our minds with.

What on earth should we men do going about with purity and innocence? A carefully thought-out buttonhole is much more effective.

The only difference between a caprice and a lifelong passion is that the caprice lasts a little longer.

People say sometimes that beauty is only superficial. That may be so, but at least it is not so superficial as thought is.

It is the spectator and not life that art really mirrors.

Nowadays people know the price of everything and the value of nothing.

Conscience and cowardice are really the same things. Conscience is the trade name of the firm—that is all.

In every sphere of life form is the beginning of things. The rhythmic, harmonious gestures of dancing convey, Plato tells us, both rhythm and harmony into the mind. Forms are the food of faith, cried Newman, in one of those great moments of sincerity that make us admire and know the man. He was right, though he may not have known how terribly right he was. The creeds are believed not because they are rational but because they are repeated. Yes; form is everything. It is the secret of life. Find expression for a sorrow and it will become dear to you. Find expression for a joy and you intensify its ecstasy. Do you wish to love? Use love's litany and the words will create the yearning from which the world fancies that they spring. Have you a grief that corrodes your heart? Learn its utterance from Prince Hamlet and Queen Constance and you will find that mere expression is a mode of consolation and that form, which is the birth of passion, is also the death of pain. And so, to return to the sphere of art, it is form that creates not merely the critical temperament but also the æsthetic instinct that reveals to one all things under the condition of beauty. Start with the worship of form and there is no secret in art that will not be revealed to you.

It is only the intellectually lost who ever argue.

Nowadays most people die of a sort of creeping common-sense, and discover when it is too late that the only things one never regrets are one's mistakes.

Lady Henry Wotton was a curious woman, whose dresses always looked as if they had been designed in a rage and put on in a tempest. She was usually in love with somebody, and, as her passion was never returned, she had kept all her illusions. She tried to look picturesque but only succeeded in being untidy.

Those who go beneath the surface do so at their peril.

With an evening coat and a white tie anybody, even a stockbroker, can gain a reputation for being civilised.

There is nothing so interesting as telling a good man or woman how bad one has been. It is intellectually fascinating. One of the greatest pleasures of having been wicked is that one has so much to say to the good.

Laws are made in order that people in authority may not remember them, just as marriages are made in order that the divorce court may not play about idly.

To get back one's youth one has merely to repeat one's follies.

Never marry a woman with straw-coloured hair. They are so sentimental.

The reason we all like to think so well of others is that we are all afraid for ourselves. The basis of optimism is sheer terror. We think that we are generous because we credit our neighbours with the possession of those virtues that are likely to be a benefit to us. We praise the banker that we may overdraw our account, and find good qualities in the high-wayman in the hope that he may spare our pockets. I have the greatest contempt for optimism.

Art begins with abstract decoration, with purely imaginative and pleasureable work dealing with what is unreal and non-existent. This is the first stage. Then life becomes fascinated with this new wonder, and asks to be admitted into the charmed circle. Art takes life as part of her rough material, recreates it and refashions it in fresh form; is absolutely indifferent to facts; invents, imagines, dreams, and keeps between herself and reality the impenetrable barrier of beautiful style, of decorative or ideal treatment. The third stage is when Life gets the upper hand and drives Art out into the wilderness. This is the true decadence, and it is from this that we are now suffering.

Good intentions have been the ruin of the world. The only people who have achieved anything have been those who have had no intentions at all.

I never take any notice of what common people say, and I never interfere with what charming people do.

You know I am not a champion of marriage. The real drawback to marriage is that it makes one unselfish, and unselfish people are colourless— they lack individuality. Still there are certain temperaments that marriage makes more complex. They retain their egotism, and add to it many other egos. They are forced to have more than one life. They become more highly organised, and to be highly organised is, I should fancy, the object of man's existence. Besides, every experience is of value, and whatever one may say against marriage it is certainly an experience.

Those who read the symbol do so at their peril.

I never talk during music—at least not during good music. If anyone hears bad music it is one's duty to drown it in conversation.

When critics disagree the artist is in accord with himself.

Faith is the most plural thing I know. We are all supposed to believe in the same thing in different ways. It is like eating out of the same dish with different coloured spoons.

Experience is of no ethical value. It is merely the name men give to their mistakes. Moralists have, as a rule, regarded it as a mode of warning, have claimed for it a certain ethical efficacy in the formation of character, have praised it as something that teaches us what to follow and shows us what to avoid. But there is no motive power in experience. It is as little of an active cause as conscience itself. All that it really demonstrates is that our future will be the same as our past and that the sin we have done once, and with loathing, we shall do many times, and with joy.

Sensations are the details that build up the stories of our lives.

No artist has ethical sympathies. An ethical sympathy in an artist is an unpardonable mannerism of style.

She looks like an 'edition de luxe' of a wicked French novel meant specially for the English market.

I never knew what terror was before; I know it now. It is as if a hand of ice were laid upon one's heart. It is as if one's heart were beating itself to death in some empty hollow.

We can forgive a man for making a useful thing as long as he does not admire it. The only excuse for making a useless thing is that one admires it intensely.

No artist desires to prove anything. Even things that are true can be proved.

One knows so well the popular idea of health. The English country gentleman galloping along after a fox—the unspeakable in pursuit of the uneatable.

People seldom tell the truths that are worth telling. We ought to choose our truths as carefully as we choose our lies and to select our virtues with as much thought as we bestow upon the selection of our enemies.

Soul and body, body and soul—how mysterious they are! There is animalism in the soul, and the body has its moments of spirituality. The senses can refine and the intellect can degrade. Who can say where the fleshly impulse ceases or the psychical impulse begins? How shallow are the arbitrary definitions of ordinary psychologists! And yet how difficult to decide between the claims of the various schools! Is the soul a shadow seated in the house of sin? Or is the body really in the soul, as Giordano Bruno thought? The separation of spirit from matter is a mystery, and the unison of spirit with matter is a mystery also.

Those who find beautiful meanings in beautiful things are the cultivated. For these there is hope.

There is no such thing as a moral or an immoral book. Books are well written or badly written-that is all.

Marriage is a sort of forcing house. It brings strange sins to fruit, and sometimes strange renunciations.

The moral life of man forms part of the subject-matter of the artist, but the morality of art consists in the perfect use of an imperfect medium.

A sense of duty is like some horrible disease. It destroys the tissues of the mind, as certain complaints destroy the tissues of the body. The catechism has a great deal to answer for.

They are the elect to whom beautiful things mean only beauty.

Those who find ugly meanings in beautiful things are corrupt without being charming. This is a fault.

Few people have sufficient strength to resist the preposterous claims of orthodoxy.

She wore far too much rouge last night and not quite enough clothes. That is always a sign of despair in a woman.

A virtue is like a city set upon a hill—it cannot be hid. We can conceal our vices if we care to—for a time at least—but a virtue will out.

Can't make out how you stand London society. The thing has gone to the dogs: a lot of damned nobodies talking about nothing.

You don't know what an existence they lead down there. It is pure, unadulterated country life. They get up early because they have so much to do, and go to bed early because they have so little to think about.

Nothing is so fatal to a personality as the keeping of promises, unless it be telling the truth.

Who cares whether Mr Ruskin's views on Turner are sound or not? What does it matter? That mighty and majestic prose of his, so fervid and so fiery coloured in its noble eloquence, so rich in its elaborate symphonic music, so sure and certain, at its best, in subtle choice of word and epithet, is, at least, as great a work of art as any of those wonderful sunsets that bleach or rot on their corrupted canvases in England's gallery—greater, indeed, one is apt to think at times, not merely because its equal beauty is more enduring but on account of the fuller variety of its appeal—soul speaking to soul in those long, cadenced lines, not through form and colour alone, though through these, indeed, completely and without loss, but with intellectual and emotional utterance, with lofty passion and with loftier thought, with imaginative insight and with poetic aim—greater, I always think, even as literature is the greater art.

Laughter is not at all a bad beginning for a friendship, and it is far the best ending for one.

Mrs Cheveley is one of those very modern women of our time who find a new scandal as becoming as a new bonnet, and air them both in the Park every afternoon at 5.30. I am sure she adores scandals, and that the sorrow of her life at present is that she can't manage to have enough of them.

The world divides actions into three classes: good actions, bad actions that you may do, and bad actions that you may not do. If you stick to the good actions you are respected by the good. If you stick to the bad actions that you may do you are respected by the bad. But if you perform the bad actions that no one may do then the good and the bad set upon you and you are lost indeed.

I choose my friends for their good looks, my acquaintances for their good characters, and my enemies for their good intellects.

The artist is the creator of beautiful things.

To me the word 'natural' means all that is middle class, all that is of the essence of Jingoism, all that is colourless and without form and void. It might be a beautiful word, but it is the most debased coin in the currency of language.

I pity any woman who is married to a man called John. She would probably never be allowed to know the entrancing pleasure of a single moment's solitude.

It is only when we have learned to love forgetfulness that we have learned the art of living.

To reveal art and conceal the artist is art's aim.

The world taken 'en masse' is a monster, crammed with prejudices, packed with prepossessions, cankered with what it calls virtues, a Puritan, a prig. And the art of life is the art of defiance. To defy—that is what we ought to live for, instead of living, as we do, to acquiesce.

Some resemblance the creative work of the critic will have to the work that has stirred him to creation, but it will be such resemblance as exists, not between nature and the mirror that the painter of landscape or figure may be supposed to hold up to her, but between nature and the work of the decorative artist. Just as on the flowerless carpets of Persia tulip and rose blossom indeed, and are lovely to look on, though they are not reproduced in visible shape or line; just as the pearl and purple of the sea shell is echoed in the church of St Mark at Venice; just as the vaulted ceiling of the wondrous chapel at Ravenna is made gorgeous by the gold and green and sapphire of the peacock's tail, though the birds of Juno fly not across it; so the critic reproduces the work that he criticises in a mode that is never imitative, and part of whose charm may really consist in the rejection of resemblance, and shows us in this way not merely the meaning but also the mystery of beauty, and by transforming each art into literature solves once for all the problem of art's unity.

Diversity of opinion about a work of art shows that the work is new, complex, and vital.

Nothing is more painful to me than to come across virtue in a person in whom I have never suspected its existence. It is like finding a needle in a bundle of hay. It pricks you. If we have virtue we should warn people of it.

The critic is he who can translate into another manner or a new material his impression of beautiful things.

Hopper is one of nature's gentlemen—the worst type of gentleman I know.

If one intends to be good one must take it up as a profession. It is quite the most engrossing one in the world.

I like Wagner's music better than anybody's. It is so loud that one can talk the whole time without other people hearing what one says.

All art is at once surface and symbol.

Childhood is one long career of innocent eavesdropping, of hearing what one ought not to hear.

The highest as the lowest form of criticism is a mode of autobiography.

The only things worth saying are those that we forget, just as the only things worth doing are those that the world is surprised at.

Maturity is one long career of saying what one ought not to say. That is the art of conversation.

Virtue is generally merely a form of deficiency, just as vice is an assertion of intellect.

People teach in order to conceal their ignorance, as people smile in order to conceal their tears.

To be unnatural is often to be great. To be natural is generally to be stupid.

To lie finely is an art, to tell the truth is to act according to nature.

People who talk sense are like people who break stones in the road: they cover one with dust and splinters.

Jesus said to man: You have a wonderful personality. Develop it. Be yourself. Don't imagine that your perfection lies in accumulating or possessing external things. Your perfection is inside of you. If only you could realise that you would not want to be rich. Ordinary riches can be stolen from a man, real riches cannot. In the treasury-house of your soul there are infinitely precious things that may not be taken from you. Try to so shape your life that external things will not harm you, and try also to get rid of personal property. It involves sordid preoccupation, endless industry, continual wrong. Personal property hinders individualism at every step.

When Jesus talks about the poor He simply means personalities, just as when He talks about the rich He simply means people who have not developed their personalities.

An echo is often more beautiful than the voice it repeats.

THE SOUL OF MAN

The chief advantage that would result from the establishment of Socialism is, undoubtedly, the fact that Socialism would relieve us from that sordid necessity of living for others which, in the present condition of things, presses so hardly upon almost everybody. In fact, scarcely anyone at all escapes.

Now and then, in the course of the century, a great man of science, like Darwin; a great poet, like Keats; a fine critical spirit, like M, Renan; a supreme artist, like Flaubert, has been able to isolate himself, to keep himself out of reach of the clamorous claims of others, to stand 'under the shelter of the wall,' as Plato puts it, and so to realise the perfection of what was in him, to his own incomparable gain, and to the incomparable and lasting gain of the whole world. These, however, are exceptions. The majority of people spoil their lives by an unhealthy and exaggerated altruism—are forced, indeed, so to spoil them. They find themselves surrounded by hideous poverty, by hideous ugliness, by hideous starvation. It is inevitable that they should be strongly moved by all this. The emotions of man are stirred more quickly than man's intelligence; and, as I pointed out some time ago in an article on the function of criticism, it is much more easy to have sympathy with suffering than it is to have sympathy with thought. Accordingly, with admirable, though misdirected intentions, they very seriously and very sentimentally set themselves to the task of remedying the evils that they see. But their remedies do not cure the disease: they merely prolong it. Indeed, their remedies are part of the disease.

They try to solve the problem of poverty, for instance, by keeping the poor alive; or, in the case of a very advanced school, by amusing the poor.

But this is not a solution: it is an aggravation of the difficulty. The proper aim is to try and reconstruct society on such a basis that poverty will be impossible. And the altruistic virtues have really prevented the carrying out of this aim. Just as the worst slave-owners were those who were kind to their slaves, and so prevented the horror of the system being realised by those who suffered from it, and understood by those who contemplated it, so, in the present state of things in England, the people who do most harm are the people who try to do most good; and at last we have had the spectacle of men who have really studied the problem and know the life-educated men who live in the East End—coming forward and imploring the community to restrain its altruistic impulses of charity, benevolence, and the like. They do so on the ground that such charity degrades and demoralises. They are perfectly right. Charity creates a multitude of sins.

There is also this to be said. It is immoral to use private property in order to alleviate the horrible evils that result from the institution of private property. It is both immoral and unfair.

Under Socialism all this will, of course, be altered. There will be no people living in fetid dens and fetid rags, and bringing up unhealthy, hunger-pinched children in the midst of impossible and absolutely repulsive surroundings. The security of society will not depend, as it does now, on the state of the weather. If a frost comes we shall not have a hundred thousand men out of work, tramping about the streets in a state of disgusting misery, or whining to their neighbours for alms, or crowding round the doors of loathsome shelters to try and secure a hunch of bread and a night's unclean lodging. Each member of the society will share in the general prosperity and happiness of the society, and if a frost comes no one will practically be anything the worse.

Upon the other hand, Socialism itself will be of value simply because it will lead to Individualism.

Socialism, Communism, or whatever one chooses to call it, by converting private property into public wealth, and substituting co-operation for competition, will restore society to its proper condition of a thoroughly healthy organism, and insure the material well-being of each member of the community. It will, in fact, give Life it's proper basis and its proper environment. But for the full development of Life to its highest mode of perfection, something more is needed. What is needed is Individualism. If the

Socialism is Authoritarian; if there are Governments armed with economic power as they are now with political power; if, in a word, we are to have Industrial Tyrannies, then the last state of man will be worse than the first. At present, in consequence of the existence of private property, a great many people are enabled to develop a certain very limited amount of Individualism. They are either under no necessity to work for their living, or are enabled to choose the sphere of activity that is really congenial to them, and gives them pleasure. These are the poets, the philosophers, the men of science, the men of culture—in a word, the real men, the men who have realised themselves, and in whom all Humanity gains a partial realisation. Upon the other hand, there are a great many people who, having no private property of their own, and being always on the brink of sheer starvation, are compelled to do the work of beasts of burden, to do work that is quite uncongenial to them, and to which they are forced by the peremptory, unreasonable, degrading Tyranny of want. These are the poor, and amongst them there is no grace of manner, or charm of speech, or civilisation, or culture, or refinement in pleasures, or joy of life. From their collective force Humanity gains much in material prosperity. But it is only the material result that it gains, and the man who is poor is in himself absolutely of no importance. He is merely the infinitesimal atom of a force that, so far from regarding him, crushes him: indeed, prefers him crushed, as in that case he is far more obedient.

Of course, it might be said that the Individualism generated under conditions of private property is not always, or even as a rule, of a fine or wonderful type, and that the poor, if they have not culture and charm, have still many virtues. Both these statements would be quite true. The possession of private property is very often extremely demoralising, and that is, of course, one of the reasons why Socialism wants to get rid of the institution. In fact, property is really a nuisance. Some years ago people went about the country saying that property has duties. They said it so often and so tediously that, at last, the Church has begun to say it. One hears it now from every pulpit. It is perfectly true. Property not merely has duties, but has so many duties that its possession to any large extent is a bore. It involves endless claims upon one, endless attention to business, endless bother. If property had simply pleasures, we could stand it; but its duties make it unbearable. In the interest of the rich we must get rid of it. The virtues of the poor may be readily admitted, and are much to be regretted. We are often told that the poor are grateful for charity. Some of them are, no doubt, but the best amongst the poor are never grateful. They are ungrateful, discontented, disobedient, and rebellious. They are quite right to be so. Charity they feel to be a ridiculously inadequate mode of partial restitution, or a sentimental dole, usually accompanied by some impertinent attempt on the part of the sentimentalist to tyrannise over their private lives. Why should they be grateful for the crumbs that fall from the rich man's table? They should be seated at the board, and are beginning to know it. As for being discontented, a man who would not be discontented with such surroundings and such a low mode of life would be a perfect brute. Disobedience, in the eyes of anyone who has read history, is man's original virtue. It is through disobedience that progress has been made, through disobedience and through rebellion. Sometimes the poor are praised for being thrifty. But to recommend thrift to the poor is both grotesque and insulting. It is like advising a man who is starving to eat less. For a town or country labourer to practise thrift would be absolutely immoral. Man should not be ready to show that he can live like a badly-fed animal. He should decline to live like that, and should either steal or go on the rates, which is considered by many to be a form of stealing. As for begging, it is safer to beg than to take, but it is finer to take than to beg. No: a poor man who is ungrateful, unthrifty, discontented, and rebellious, is probably a real personality, and has much in him. He is at any rate a healthy protest. As for the virtuous poor, one can pity them, of course, but one cannot possibly admire them; They have made private terms with the enemy, and sold their birthright for very bad pottage. They must also be extraordinarily stupid. I can quite understand a man accepting laws that protect private property, and admit of its accumulation, as long as he himself is able under those conditions to realise some form of beautiful and intellectual life. But it is almost incredible to me how a man whose life is marred and made hideous by such laws can possibly acquiesce in their continuance.

However, the explanation is not really difficult to find. It is simply this. Misery and poverty are so absolutely degrading, and exercise such a paralysing effect over the nature of men, that no class is ever really conscious of its own suffering. They have to be told of it by other people, and they often entirely disbelieve them. What is said by great employers of labour against agitators is unquestionably true. Agitators are a set of interfering, meddling people, who come down to some perfectly contented class of the community, and sow the seeds of discontent amongst them. That is the reason why agitators are so absolutely necessary. Without them, in our incomplete state, there would be no advance towards civilisation. Slavery was put down in America, not in consequence of any action on the part of the slaves, or even any express desire on their part that they should be free. It was put down entirely through the grossly illegal conduct of certain agitators in Boston and elsewhere, who were not slaves themselves, nor owners of slaves, nor had anything to do with the question really. It was, undoubtedly, the Abolitionists who set the torch alight, who began the whole thing. And it is curious to note that from the slaves themselves they received, not merely very little assistance, but hardly any sympathy even; and when at the close of the war the slaves found themselves free, found themselves indeed so absolutely free that they were free to starve, many of them bitterly regretted the new state of things. To the thinker, the most tragic fact in the whole of the French Revolution is not that Marie Antoinette was killed for being a queen, but that the starved peasant of the Vendée voluntarily went out to die for the hideous cause of feudalism.

It is clear, then, that no Authoritarian Socialism will do. For while under the present system a very large number of people can lead lives of a certain amount of freedom and expression and happiness, under an industrial-barrack system, or a system of economic tyranny, nobody would be able to have any such freedom at all. It is to be regretted that a portion of our community should be practically in slavery, but to propose to solve the problem by enslaving the entire community is childish. Every man must be left quite free to choose his own work. No form of compulsion must be exercised over him. If there is, his work will not be good for him, will riot be good in itself, and will not be good for others. And by work I simply mean activity of any kind.

I hardly think that any Socialist, nowadays, would seriously propose that an inspector should call every morning at each house to see that each citizen rose up and did manual labour for eight hours. Humanity has got beyond that stage, and reserves such a form of life for the people whom, in a very arbitrary manner, it chooses to call criminals. But I confess that many of the socialistic views that I have come across seem to me to be tainted with ideas of authority, if not of actual compulsion. Of course, authority and compulsion are out of the question. All association must be quite voluntary. It is only in voluntary associations that man is fine.

But it may be asked how Individualism, which is now more or less dependent on the existence of private property for its development, will benefit by the abolition of such private property. The answer is very simple. It is true that, under existing conditions, a few men who have had private means of their own, such as Byron, Shelley, Browning, Victor Hugo, Baudelaire, and others, have been able to realise their personality more or less completely. Not one of these men ever did a single day's work for hire. They were relieved from poverty. They had an immense advantage. The question is whether it would be for the good of Individualism that such an advantage should be taken away. Let us suppose that it is taken away. What happens then to Individualism? How will it benefit?

It will benefit in this way, under the new conditions Individualism will be far freer, far finer, and far more intensified than it is now. I am not talking of the great imaginatively-realised Individualism of such poets as I have mentioned, but of the great actual Individualism latent and potential in mankind generally. For the recognition of private property has really harmed Individualism, and obscured it, by confusing a man with what he possesses. It has led Individualism entirely astray. It has made gain not growth its aim. So that man thought that the important thing was to have, and did not know that the important thing is to be. The true perfection of man lies, not in what man has, but in what man is. Private property has crushed true Individualism, and set up an Individualism that is false. It has debarred one part of the community from being individual by starving them. It has debarred the other part of the community from being individual by putting them on the wrong road, and encumbering them. Indeed, so completely has man's personality been absorbed by his possessions that the English law has always treated offences against a man's property with far more severity than offences against his person, and property is still the test of complete citizenship. The industry necessary for the making of money is also very demoralising. In a community like ours, where property confers immense distinction, social position, honour, respect, titles, and other pleasant things of the kind, man, being naturally ambitious, makes it his aim to accumulate this property, and goes on wearily and tediously accumulating it long after he has got far more than he wants, or can use, or enjoy, or perhaps even know of. Man will kill himself by overwork in order to secure property, and really, considering the enormous advantages that property brings, one is hardly surprised. One's regret is that society should be constructed on such a basis that man has been forced into a groove in which he cannot freely develop what is wonderful, and fascinating, and delightful in him—in which, in fact, he misses the true pleasure and joy of living. He is also, under existing conditions, very insecure. An enormously wealthy merchant may be—often is—at every moment of his life at the mercy of things that are not under his control. If the wind blows an extra point or so, or the weather suddenly changes, or some trivial thing happens, his ship may go down, his speculations may go wrong, and he finds himself a poor man, with his social position quite gone. Now, nothing should be able to harm a man except himself. Nothing should be able to rob a man at all. What a man really has, is what is in him. What is outside of him should be a matter of no importance.

With the abolition of private property, then, we shall have true, beautiful, healthy Individualism. Nobody will waste his life in accumulating things, and the symbols for things. One will live. To live is the rarest thing in the world. Most people exist, that is all.

It is a question whether we have ever seen the full expression of a personality, except on the imaginative plane of art. In action, we never have. Cæsar, says Mommsen, was the complete and perfect man. But how tragically insecure was Cæsar! Wherever there is a man who exercises authority, there is a man who resists authority. Cæsar was very perfect, but his perfection travelled by too dangerous a road. Marcus Aurelius was the perfect man, says Renan. Yes; the great emperor was a perfect man. But how intolerable were the endless claims upon him! He staggered under the burden of the empire.

He was conscious how inadequate one man was to bear the weight of that Titan and too vast orb. What I mean by a perfect man is one who develops under perfect conditions; one who is not wounded, or worried or maimed, or in danger. Most personalities have been obliged to be rebels. Half their strength has been wasted in friction. Byron's personality, for instance, was terribly wasted in its battle with the stupidity, and hypocrisy, and Philistinism of the English. Such battles do not always intensify strength: they often exaggerate weakness. Byron was never able to give us what he might have given us. Shelley escaped better. Like Byron, he got out of England as soon as possible. But he was not so well known. If the English had had any idea of what a great poet he really was, they would have fallen on him with tooth and nail, and made his life as unbearable to him as they possibly could. But he was not a remarkable figure in society, and consequently he escaped, to a certain degree. Still, even in Shelley the note of rebellion is sometimes too strong. The note of the perfect personality is not rebellion, but peace.

It will be a marvellous thing—the true personality of man—when we see it. It will grow naturally and simply, flowerlike, or as a tree grows. It will not be at discord. It will never argue or dispute. It will not prove things. It will know everything. And yet it will not busy itself about knowledge. It will have wisdom. Its value will not be measured by material things. It will have nothing. And yet it will have everything, and whatever one takes from it, it will still have, so rich will it he. It will not be always meddling with others, or asking them to be like itself. It will love them because they will be different. And yet while it will not meddle with others, it will help all, as a beautiful thing helps us, by being what it is. The personality of man will be very wonderful. It will be as wonderful as the personality of a child.

In its development it will be assisted by Christianity, if men desire that; but if men do not desire that, it will develop none the less surely. For it will not worry itself about the past, nor care whether things happened or did not happen. Nor will it admit any laws but its own laws; nor any authority but its own authority. Yet it will love those who sought to intensity it, and speak often of them. And of these Christ was one.

'Know thyself' was written over the portal of the antique world. Over the portal of the new world, 'Be thyself' shall be written. And the message of Christ to man was simply 'Be thyself.' That is the secret of Christ.

When Jesus talks about the poor he simply means personalities, just as when he talks about the rich he simply means people who have not developed their personalities. Jesus moved in a community that allowed the accumulation of private property just as ours does, and the gospel that he preached was not that in such a community it is an advantage for a man to live on scanty, unwholesome food, to wear ragged, unwholesome clothes, to sleep in horrid, unwholesome dwellings, and a disadvantage for a man to live under healthy, pleasant, and decent conditions. Such a view would have been wrong there and then, and would, of course, be still more wrong now and in England; for as man moves northward the material necessities of life become of more vital importance, and our society is infinitely more complex, and displays far greater extremes of luxury and pauperism than any society of the antique world. What Jesus meant, was this. He said to man, 'You have a wonderful personality. Develop it. Be yourself. Don't imagine that your perfection lies in accumulating or possessing external things. Your perfection is inside of you. If only you could realise that, you would not want to be rich. Ordinary riches can be stolen from a man. Real riches cannot. In the treasury-house of your soul, there are infinitely precious things, that may not be taken from you. And so, try to so shape your life that external things will not harm you. And try also to get rid of personal property. It involves sordid preoccupation, endless industry, continual wrong. Personal property hinders Individualism at every step. It is to be noted that Jesus never says that impoverished people are necessarily good, or wealthy people necessarily bad. That would not have been true. Wealthy people are, as a class, better than impoverished people, more moral, more intellectual, more well-behaved. There is only one class in the community that thinks more about money than the rich, and that is the poor. The poor can think of nothing else. That is the misery of being poor. What Jesus does say is that man reaches his perfection, not through what he has, not even through what he does, but entirely through what he is. And so the wealthy young man who comes to Jesus is represented as a thoroughly good citizen, who has broken none of the laws of his state, none of the commandments of his religion. He is quite respectable, in the ordinary sense of that extraordinary word. Jesus says to him, 'You should give up private property. It hinders you from realising your perfection. It is a drag upon you. It is a burden. Your personality does not need it. It is within you, and not outside of you, that you will find what you really are, and what you really want.' To his own friends he says the same thing. He tells them to be themselves, and not to be always worrying about other things. What do other things matter? Man is complete in himself. When they go into the world, the world will disagree with them. That is inevitable. The world hates Individualism. But that is not to trouble them. They are to be calm and self-centred. If a man takes their cloak, they are to give him their coat, just to show that material things are of no importance. If people abuse them, they are not to answer back. What does it signify? The things people say of a man do not alter a man. He is what he is. Public opinion is of no value whatsoever. Even if people employ actual violence, they are not to be violent in turn. That would be to fall to the same low level. After all, even in prison, a man can be quite free. His soul can be free. His personality can be untroubled. He can be at peace. And, above all things, they are not to interfere with other people or judge them in any way. Personality is a very mysterious thing. A man cannot always be estimated by what he does. He may keep the law, and yet be worthless. He may break the law, and yet be fine. He may be bad, without ever doing anything bad. He may commit a sin against society, and yet realise through that sin his true perfection.

There was a woman who was taken in adultery. We are not told the history of her love, but that love must have been very great; for Jesus said that her sins were forgiven her, not because she repented, but because her love was so intense and wonderful. Later on, a short time before his death, as he sat at a feast, the woman came in and poured costly perfumes on his hair. His friends tried to interfere with her, and said that it was an extravagance, and that the money that the perfume cost should have been expended on charitable relief of people in want, or something of that kind. Jesus did not accept that view. He pointed out that the material needs of Man were great and very permanent, but that the spiritual needs of Man were greater still, and that in one divine moment, and by selecting its own mode of expression, a personality might make itself perfect. The world worships the woman, even now, as a saint.

Yes; there are suggestive things in Individualism. Socialism annihilates family life, for instance. With the abolition of private property, marriage in its present form must disappear. This is part of the programme. Individualism accepts this and makes it fine. It converts the abolition of legal restraint into a form of freedom that will help the full development of personality, and make the love of man and woman more wonderful, more beautiful, and more ennobling. Jesus knew this. He rejected the claims of family life, although they existed in his day and community in a very marked form. 'Who is my mother? Who are my brothers?' he said, when he was told that they wished to speak to him. When one of his followers asked leave to go and bury his father, 'Let the dead bury the dead,' was his terrible answer. He would allow no claim whatsoever to be made on personality.

And so he who would lead a Christ-like like life is he who is perfectly and absolutely himself. He may be a great poet, or a great man of science; or a young student at a University, or one who watches sheep upon a moor; or a maker of dramas, like Shakespeare, or a thinker about God, like Spinoza; or a child who plays in a garden, or a fisherman who throws his net into the sea. It does not matter what he is, as long as he realises the perfection of the soul that is within him. All imitation in morals and in life is wrong. Through the streets of Jerusalem at the present day crawls one who is mad and carries a wooden cross on his shoulders. He is a symbol of the lives that are marred by imitation. Father Damien was Christ-like when he went out to live with the lepers, because in such service he realised fully what was best in him. But he was not more Christ-like than Wagner when he realised his soul in music; or than Shelley, when he realised his soul in song. There is no one type for man. There are as many perfections as there are imperfect men. And while to the claims of charity a man may yield and yet be free, to the claims of conformity no man may yield and remain free at all.

Individualism, then, is what through Socialism we are to attain to. As a natural result the State must give up all idea of government. It must give it up because, as a wise man once said many centuries before Christ, there is such a thing as leaving mankind alone; there is no such thing as governing mankind. All modes of government are failures. Despotism is unjust to everybody, including the despot, who was probably made for better things. Oligarchies are unjust to the many, and ochlocracies are unjust to the few. High hopes were once formed of democracy; but democracy means simply the bludgeoning of the people by the people for the people. It has been found out. I must say that it was high time, for all authority is quite degrading. It degrades those who exercise it, and degrades those over whom it is exercised. When it is violently, grossly, and cruelly used, it produces a good effect, by creating, or at any rate bringing out, the spirit of revolt and Individualism that is to kill it. When it is used with a certain amount of kindness, and accompanied by prizes and rewards, it is dreadfully demoralising. People, in that case, are less conscious of the horrible pressure that is being put on them, and so go through their lives in a sort of coarse comfort, like petted animals, without ever realising that they are probably thinking other people's thoughts, living by other people's standards, wearing practically what one may call other people's second-hand clothes, and never being themselves for a single moment. 'He who would be free,' says a fine thinker, 'must not conform.' And authority, by bribing people to conform, produces a very gross kind of over-fed barbarism amongst us.

With authority, punishment will pass away. This will be a great gain—a gain, in fact, of incalculable value. As one reads history, not in the expurgated editions written for schoolboys and passmen, but in the original authorities of each time, one is absolutely sickened, not by the crimes that the wicked have committed, but by the punishments that the good have inflicted; and a community is infinitely more brutalised by the habitual employment of punishment, than it is by the occurrence of crime. It obviously follows that the more punishment is inflicted the more crime is produced, and most modern legislation has clearly recognised this, and has made it its task to diminish punishment as far as it thinks it can. Wherever it has really diminished it, the results have always been extremely good. The less punishment, the less crime. When there is no punishment at all, crime will either cease to exist, or, if it occurs, will be treated by physicians as a very distressing form of dementia, to be cured by care and kindness. For what are called criminals nowadays are not criminals at all. Starvation, and not sin, is the parent of modern crime. That indeed is the reason why our criminals are, as a class, so absolutely uninteresting from any psychological point of view. They are not marvellous Macbeths and terrible Vautrins. They are merely what ordinary, respectable, commonplace people would be if they had not got enough to eat. When private property is abolished there will be no necessity for crime, no demand for it; it will cease to exist. Of course, all crimes are not crimes against property, though such are the crimes that the English law, valuing what a man has more than what a man is, punishes with the harshest and most horrible severity, if we except the crime of murder, and regard death as worse than penal servitude, a point on which our criminals, I believe, disagree. But though a crime may not be against property, it may spring from the misery and rage and depression produced by our wrong system of property-holding, and so, when that system is abolished, will disappear. When each member of the community has sufficient for his wants, and is not interfered with by his neighbour, it will not be an object of any interest to him to interfere with anyone else. Jealousy, which is an extraordinary source of crime in modern life, is an emotion closely bound up with our conceptions of property, and under Socialism and Individualism will die out. It is remarkable that in communistic tribes jealousy is entirely unknown.

Now as the State is not to govern, it may be asked what the State is to do. The State is to be a voluntary association that will organise labour, and be the manufacturer and distributor of necessary commodities. The State is to make what is useful. The individual is to make what is beautiful. And as I have mentioned the word labour, I cannot help saying that a great deal of nonsense is being written and talked nowadays about the dignity of manual labour. There is nothing necessarily dignified about manual labour at all, and most of it is absolutely degrading. It is mentally and morally injurious to man to do anything in which he does not find pleasure, and many forms of labour are quite pleasureless activities, and should be regarded as such. To sweep a slushy crossing for eight hours on a day when the east wind is blowing is a disgusting occupation. To sweep it with mental, moral, or physical dignity seems to me to be impossible. To sweep it with joy would be appalling. Man is made for something better than disturbing dirt. All work of that kind should be done by a machine.

And I have no doubt that it will be so. Up to the present, man has been, to a certain extent, the slave of machinery, and there is something tragic in the fact that as soon as man had invented a machine to do his work he began to starve. This, however, is, of course, the result of our property system and our system of competition. One man owns a machine which does the work of five hundred men. Five hundred men are, in consequence, thrown out of employment, and, having no work to do, become hungry and take to thieving. The one man secures the produce of the machine and keeps it, and has five hundred times as much as he should have, and probably, which is of much more importance, a great deal more than he really wants. Were that machine the property of all, everyone would benefit by it. It would be an immense advantage to the community. All unintellectual labour, all monotonous, dull labour, all labour that deals with dreadful things, and involves unpleasant conditions, must be done by machinery. Machinery must work for us in coal mines, and do all sanitary services, and be the stoker of steamers, and clean the streets, and run messages on wet days, and do anything that is tedious or distressing. At present machinery competes against man. Under proper conditions machinery will serve man. There is no doubt at all that this is the future of machinery, and just as trees grow while the country gentleman is asleep, so while Humanity will be amusing itself, or enjoying cultivated leisure—which, and not labour, is the aim of man—or making beautiful things, or reading beautiful things, or simply contemplating the world with admiration and delight, machinery will he doing all the necessary and unpleasant work. The fact is, that civilisation requires slaves. The Greeks were quite right there. Unless there are slaves to do the ugly, horrible, uninteresting work, culture and contemplation become almost impossible. Human slavery is wrong, insecure, and demoralising. On mechanical slavery, on the slavery of the machine, the future of the world depends. And when scientific men are no longer called upon to go down to a depressing East End and distribute bad cocoa and worse blankets to starving people, they will have delightful leisure in which to devise wonderful and marvellous things for their own joy and the joy of everyone else. There will be great storages of force for every city, and for every house if required, and this force man will convert into heat, light, or motion, according to his needs. Is this Utopian? A map of the world that does not include Utopia is not worth even glancing at, for it leaves out the one country at which Humanity is always landing. And when Humanity lands there, it looks out, and, seeing a better country, sets sail. Progress is the realisation of Utopias.

Now, I have said that the community by means of organisation of machinery will supply the useful things, and that the beautiful things will be made by the individual. This is not merely necessary, but it is the only possible way by which we can get either the one or the other. An individual who has to make things for the use of others, and with reference to their wants and their wishes, does not work with interest, and consequently cannot put into his work what is best in him. Upon the other hand, whenever a community or a powerful section of a community, or a government of any kind, attempts to dictate to the artist what he is to do, Art either entirely vanishes, or becomes stereotyped, or degenerates into a low and ignoble form of craft. A work of art is the unique result of a unique temperament. Its beauty comes from the fact that the author is what he is. It has nothing to do with the fact that other people want what they want. Indeed, the moment that an artist takes notice of what other people want, and tries to supply the demand, he ceases to be an artist, and becomes a dull or an amusing craftsman, an honest or a dishonest tradesman. He has no further claim to be considered as an artist. Art is the most intense mode of Individualism that the world has known. I am inclined to say that it is the only real mode of Individualism that the world has known. Crime, which, under certain conditions, may seem to have created Individualism, must take cognisance of other people and interfere with them. It belongs to the sphere of action. But alone, without any reference to his neighbours, without any interference, the artist can fashion a beautiful thing; and if he does not do it solely for his own pleasure, he is not an artist at all.

And it is to be noted that it is the fact that Art is this intense form of Individualism that makes the public try to exercise over it an authority that is as immoral as it is ridiculous, and as corrupting as it is contemptible. It is not quite their fault. The public has always, and in every age, been badly brought up. They are continually asking Art to be popular, to please their want of taste, to flatter their absurd vanity, to tell them what they have been told before, to show them what they ought to be tired of seeing, to amuse them when they feel heavy after eating too much, and to distract their thoughts when they are wearied of their own stupidity. Now Art should never try to be popular. The public should try to make itself artistic. There is a very wide difference. If a man of science were told that the results of his experiments, and the conclusions that he arrived at, should be of such a character that they would not upset the received popular notions on the subject, or disturb popular prejudice, or hurt the sensibilities of people who knew nothing about science; if a philosopher were told that he had a perfect right to speculate in the highest spheres of thought, provided that he arrived at the same conclusions as were held by those who had never thought in any sphere at all—well, nowadays the man of science and the philosopher would be considerably amused. Yet it is really a very few years since both philosophy and science were subjected to brutal popular control, to authority in fact—the authority of either the general ignorance of the community, or the terror and greed for power of an ecclesiastical or governmental class. Of course, we have to a very great extent got rid of any attempt on the part of the community, or the Church, or the Government, to interfere with the individualism of speculative thought, but the attempt to interfere with the individualism of imaginative art still lingers. In fact, it does more than linger; it is aggressive, offensive, and brutalising.

In England, the arts that have escaped best are the arts in which the public take no interest. Poetry is an instance of what I mean. We have been able to have fine poetry in England because the public do not read it, and consequently do not influence it. The public like to insult poets because they are individual, but once they have insulted them, they leave them alone. In the case of the novel and the drama, arts in which the public do take an interest, the result of the exercise of popular authority has been absolutely ridiculous. No country produces such badly-written fiction, such tedious, common work in the novel form, such silly, vulgar plays as England. It must necessarily be so. The popular standard is of such a character that no artist can get to it. It is at once too easy and too difficult to be a popular novelist. It is too easy, because the requirements of the public as far as plot, style, psychology, treatment of life, and treatment of literature are concerned are within the reach of the very meanest capacity and the most uncultivated mind. It is too difficult, because to meet such requirements the artist would have to do violence to his temperament, would have to write not for the artistic joy of writing, but for the amusement of half-educated people, and so would have to suppress his individualism, forget his culture, annihilate his style, and surrender everything that is valuable in him. In the case of the drama, things are a little better: the theatre-going public like the obvious, it is true, but they do not like the tedious; and burlesque and farcical comedy, the two most popular forms, are distinct forms of art. Delightful work may be produced under burlesque and farcical conditions, and in work of this kind the artist in England is allowed very great freedom. It is when one comes to the higher forms of the drama that the result of popular control is seen. The one thing that the public dislike is novelty. Any attempt to extend the subject-matter of art is extremely distasteful to the public; and yet the vitality and progress of art depend in a large measure on the continual extension of subject-matter. The public dislike novelty because they are afraid of it. It represents to them a mode of Individualism, an assertion on the part of the artist that he selects his own subject, and treats it as he chooses. The public are quite right in their attitude. Art is Individualism, and Individualism is a disturbing and disintegrating force. Therein lies its immense value. For what it seeks to disturb is monotony of type, slavery of custom, tyranny of habit, and the reduction of man to the level of a machine. In Art, the public accept what has been, because they cannot alter it, not because they appreciate it. They swallow their classics whole, and never taste them. They endure them as the inevitable, and as they cannot mar them, they mouth about them. Strangely enough, or not strangely, according to one's own views, this acceptance of the classics does a great deal of harm. The uncritical admiration of the Bible and Shakespeare in England is an instance of what I mean. With regard to the Bible, considerations of ecclesiastical authority enter into the matter, so that I need not dwell upon the point.

But in the case of Shakespeare it is quite obvious that the public really see neither the beauties nor the defects of his plays. If they saw the beauties, they would not object to the development of the drama; and if they saw the defects, they would not object to the development of the drama either. The fact is, the public make use of the classics of a country as a means of checking the progress of Art. They degrade the classics into authorities. They use them as bludgeons for preventing the free expression of Beauty in new forms. They are always asking a writer why he does not write like somebody else, or a painter why he does not paint like somebody else, quite oblivious of the fact that if either of them did anything of the kind he would cease to be an artist. A fresh mode of Beauty is absolutely distasteful to them, and whenever it appears they get so angry and bewildered, that they always use two stupid expressions—one is that the work of art is grossly unintelligible; the other, that the work of art is grossly immoral. What they mean by these words seems to me to be this. When they say a work is grossly unintelligible, they mean that the artist has said or made a beautiful thing that is new; when they describe a work as grossly immoral, they mean that the artist has said or made a beautiful thing that is true. The former expression has reference to style; the latter to subject-matter. But they probably use the words very vaguely, as an ordinary mob will use ready-made paving-stones. There is not a single real poet or prose-writer of this century, for instance, on whom the British public have not solemnly conferred diplomas of immorality, and these diplomas practically take the place, with us, of what in France, is the formal recognition of an Academy of Letters, and fortunately make the establishment of such an institution quite unnecessary in England. Of course, the public are very reckless in their use of the word. That they should have called Wordsworth an immoral poet, was only to be expected. Wordsworth was a poet. But that they should have called Charles Kingsley an immoral novelist is extraordinary. Kingsley's prose was not of a very fine quality. Still, there is the word, and they use it as best they can. An artist is, of course, not disturbed by it. The true artist is a man who believes absolutely in himself, because he is absolutely himself. But I can fancy that if an artist produced a work of art in England that immediately on its appearance was recognised by the public, through their medium, which is the public press, as a work that was quite intelligible and highly moral, he would begin to seriously question whether in its creation he had really been himself at all, and consequently whether the work was not quite unworthy of him, and either of a thoroughly second-rate order, or of no artistic value whatsoever.

Perhaps, however, I have wronged the public in limiting them to

84

such words as 'immoral,' 'unintelligible,' 'exotic,' and 'unhealthy.' There is one other word that they use. That word is 'morbid.' They do not use it often. The meaning of the word is so simple that they are afraid of using it. Still, they use it sometimes, and, now and then, one comes across it in popular newspapers. It is, of course, a ridiculous word to apply to a work of art. For what is morbidity but a mood of emotion or a mode of thought that one cannot express? The public are all morbid, because the public can never find expression for anything. The artist is never morbid. He expresses everything. He stands outside his subject, and through its medium produces incomparable and artistic effects. To call an artist morbid because he deals with morbidity as his subject-matter is as silly as if one called Shakespeare mad because he wrote 'King Lear.'

On the whole, an artist in England gains something by being attacked. His individuality is intensified. He becomes more completely himself. Of course, the attacks are very gross, very impertinent, and very contemptible. But then no artist expects grace from the vulgar mind, or style from the suburban intellect. Vulgarity and stupidity are two very vivid facts in modern life. One regrets them, naturally. But there they are. They are subjects for study, like everything else. And it is only fair to state, with regard to modern journalists, that they always apologise to one in private for what they have written against one in public.

Within the last few years two other adjectives, it may be mentioned, have been added to the very limited vocabulary of art-abuse that is at the disposal of the public. One is the word 'unhealthy,' the other is the word 'exotic.' The latter merely expresses the rage of the momentary mushroom against the immortal, entrancing, and exquisitely lovely orchid. It is a tribute, but a tribute of no importance. The word 'unhealthy,' however, admits of analysis. It is a rather interesting word. In fact, it is so interesting that the people who use it do not know what it means.

What does it mean? What is a healthy, or an unhealthy work of art? All terms that one applies to a work of art, provided that one applies them rationally, have reference to either its style or its subject, or to both together. From the point of view of style, a healthy work of art is one whose style recognises the beauty of the material it employs, be that material one of words or of bronze, of colour or of ivory, and uses that beauty as a factor in producing the æsthetic effect. From the point of view of subject, a healthy work of art is one the choice of whose subject is conditioned by the temperament of the artist, and comes directly out of it. In fine, a healthy work of art is one that has both perfection and personality. Of course, form and substance cannot be separated in a work of art; they are always one. But for purposes of analysis, and setting the wholeness of æsthetic impression aside for a moment, we can intellectually so separate them. An unhealthy work of art, on the other hand, is a work whose style is obvious, old-fashioned, and common, and whose subject is deliberately chosen, not because the artist has any pleasure in it, but because he thinks that the public will pay him for it. In fact, the popular novel that the public calls healthy is always a thoroughly unhealthy production; and what the public call an unhealthy novel is always a beautiful and healthy work of art.

I need hardly say that I am not, for a single moment, complaining that the public and the public press misuse these words. I do not see how, with their lack of comprehension of what Art is, they could possibly use them in the proper sense. I am merely pointing out the misuse; and as for the origin of the misuse and the meaning that lies behind it all, the explanation is very simple. It comes from the barbarous conception of authority. It comes from the natural inability of a community corrupted by authority to understand or appreciate Individualism. In a word, it comes from that monstrous and ignorant thing that is called Public Opinion, which, bad and well-meaning as it is when it tries to control action, is infamous and of evil meaning when it tries to control Thought or Art.

Indeed, there is much more to be said in favour of the physical force of the public than there is in favour of the public's opinion. The former may be fine. The latter must be foolish. It is often said that force is no argument. That, however, entirely depends on what one wants to prove. Many of the most important problems of the last few centuries, such as the continuance of personal government in England, or of feudalism in France, have been solved entirely by means of physical force. The very violence of a revolution may make the public grand and splendid for a moment. It was a fatal day when the public discovered that the pen is mightier than the paving-stone, and can be made as offensive as the brickbat. They at once sought for the journalist, found him, developed him, and made him their industrious and well-paid servant. It is greatly to be regretted, for both their sakes. Behind the barricade there may be much that is noble and heroic. But what is there behind the leading-article but prejudice, stupidity, cant, and twaddle? And when these four are joined together they make a terrible force, and constitute the new authority.

In old days men had the rack. Now they have the press. That is an improvement certainly. But still it is very bad, and wrong, and demoralising. Somebody—was it Burke?—called journalism the fourth estate. That was true at the time, no doubt. But at the present moment it really is the only estate. It has eaten up the other three. The Lords Temporal say nothing, the Lords Spiritual have nothing to say, and the House of Commons has nothing to say and says it. We are dominated by Journalism. In America the President reigns for four years, and Journalism governs for ever and ever. Fortunately in America Journalism has carried its authority to the grossest and most brutal extreme. As a natural consequence it has begun to create a spirit of revolt. People are amused by it, or disgusted by it, according to their temperaments. But it is no longer the real force it was. It is not seriously treated. In England, Journalism, not, except in a few well-known instances, having been carried to such excesses of brutality, is still a great factor, a really remarkable power. The tyranny that it proposes to exercise over people's private lives seems to me to be quite extraordinary. The fact is, that the public have an insatiable curiosity to know everything, except what is worth knowing. Journalism, conscious of this, and having tradesman-like habits, supplies their demands. In centuries before ours the public nailed the ears of journalists to the pump. That was quite hideous. In this century journalists have nailed their own ears to the keyhole. That is much worse. And what aggravates the mischief is that the journalists who are most to blame are not the amusing journalists who write for what are called Society papers. The harm is done by the serious, thoughtful, earnest journalists, who solemnly, as they are doing at present, will drag before the eyes of the public some incident in the private life of a great statesman, of a man who is a leader of political thought as he is a creator of political force, and invite the public to discuss the incident, to exercise authority in the matter, to give their views, and not merely to give their views, but to carry them into action, to dictate to the man upon all other points, to dictate to his party, to dictate to his country; in fact, to make themselves ridiculous, offensive, and harmful. The private lives of men and women should not be told to the public. The public have nothing to do with them at all. In Prance they manage these things better. There they do not allow the details of the trials that take place in the divorce courts to be published for the amusement or criticism of the public. All that the public are allowed to know is that the divorce has taken place and was granted on petition of one or other or both of the married parties concerned. In France, in fact, they limit the journalist, and allow the artist almost perfect freedom. Here we allow absolute freedom to the journalist, and entirely limit the artist. English public opinion, that is to say, tries to constrain and impede and warp the man who makes things that are beautiful in effect, and compels the journalist to retail things that are ugly, or disgusting, or revolting in fact, so that we have the most serious journalists in the world, and the most indecent newspapers. It is no exaggeration to talk of compulsion. There are possibly some journalists who take a real pleasure in publishing horrible things, or who, being poor, look to scandals as forming a sort of permanent basis for an income. But there are other journalists, I feel certain, men of education and cultivation, who really dislike publishing these things, who know that it is wrong to do so, and only do it because the unhealthy conditions under which their occupation is carried on oblige them to supply the public with what the public wants, and to compete with other journalists in making that supply as full and satisfying to the gross popular appetite as possible. It is a very degrading position for any body of educated men to be placed in, and I have no doubt that most of them feel it acutely.

However, let us leave what is really a very sordid side of the subject, and return to the question of popular control in the matter of Art, by which I mean Public Opinion dictating to the artist the form which he is to use, the mode in which he is to use it, and the materials with which he is to work. I have pointed out that the arts which have escaped best in England are the arts in which the public have not been interested. They are, however, interested in the drama, and as a certain advance has been made in the drama within the last ten or fifteen years, it is important to point out that this advance is entirely due to a few individual artists refusing to accept the popular want of taste as their standard, and refusing to regard Art as a mere matter of demand and supply. With his marvellous and vivid personality, with a style that has really a true colour-element in it, with his extraordinary power, not over mere mimicry but over imaginative and intellectual creation, Mr Irving, had his sole object been to give the public what they wanted, could have produced the commonest plays in the commonest manner, and made as much success and money as a man could possibly desire. But his object was not that. His object was to realise his own perfection as an artist, under certain conditions, and in certain forms of Art. At first he appealed to the few; now he has educated the many. He has created in the public both taste and temperament. The public appreciate his artistic success immensely. I often wonder, however, whether the public understand that that success is entirely due to the fact that he did not accept their standard, but realised his own. With their standard the Lyceum would have been a sort of second-rate booth, as some of the popular theatres in London are at present. Whether they understand it or not the fact however remains, that taste and temperament have, to a certain extent, been created in the public, and that the public is capable of developing these qualities. The problem then is, why do not the public become more civilised? They have the capacity. What stops them?

The thing that stops them, it must be said again, is their desire to exercise authority over the artist and over works of art. To certain theatres, such as the Lyceum and the Haymarket, the public seem to come in a proper mood. In both of these theatres there have been individual artists, who have succeeded in creating in their audiences—and every theatre in London has its own audience—the temperament to which Art appeals. And what is that temperament? It is the temperament of receptivity. That is all.

If a man approaches a work of art with any desire to exercise authority over it and the artist, he approaches it in such a spirit that he cannot receive any artistic impression from it at all. The work of art is to dominate the spectator: the spectator is not to dominate the work of art. The spectator is to be receptive. He is to be the violin on which the master is to play. And the more completely he can suppress his own silly views, his own foolish prejudices, his own absurd ideas of what Art should be, or should not be, the more likely he is to understand and appreciate the work of art in question. This is, of course, quite obvious in the case of the vulgar theatre-going public of English men and women. But it is equally true of what are called educated people. For an educated person's ideas of Art are drawn naturally from what Art has been, whereas the new work of art is beautiful by being what Art has never been; and to measure it by the standard of the past is to measure it by a standard on the rejection of which its real perfection depends. A temperament capable of receiving, through an imaginative medium, and under imaginative conditions, new and beautiful impressions, is the only temperament that can appreciate a work of art. And true as this is in the case of the appreciation of sculpture and painting, it is still more true of the appreciation of such arts as the drama. For a picture and a statue are not at war with Time. They take no count of its succession. In one moment their unity may be apprehended. In the case of literature it is different. Time must be traversed before the unity of effect is realised. And so, in the drama, there may occur in the first act of the play something whose real artistic value may not be evident to the spectator till the third or fourth act is reached. Is the silly fellow to get angry and call out, and disturb the play, and annoy the artists? No, the honest man is to sit quietly, and know the delightful emotions of wonder, curiosity, and suspense. He is not to go to the play to lose a vulgar temper. He is to go to the play to realise an artistic temperament. He is to go to the play to gain an artistic temperament. He is not the arbiter of the work of art. He is one who is admitted to contemplate the work of art, and, if the work be fine, to forget in its contemplation all, the egotism that mars him—the egotism of his ignorance, or the egotism of his information. This point about the drama is hardly, I think, sufficiently recognised. I can quite understand that were 'Macbeth' produced for the first time before a modern London audience, many of the people present would strongly and vigorously object to the introduction of the witches in the first act, with their grotesque phrases and their ridiculous words. But when the play is over one realises that the laughter of the witches in 'Macbeth' is as terrible as the laughter of madness in 'Lear,' more terrible than the daughter of Iago in the tragedy of the Moor. No spectator of art needs a more perfect mood of receptivity than the spectator of a play. The moment he seeks to exercise authority he becomes the avowed enemy of Art and of himself. Art does not mind. It is he who suffers.

With the novel it is the same thing. Popular authority and the recognition of popular authority are fatal. Thackeray's 'Esmond' is a beautiful work of art because he wrote it to please himself. In his other novels, in 'Pendennis,' in 'Philip,' in 'Vanity Fair' even, at times, he is too conscious of the public, and spoils his work by appealing directly to the sympathies of the public, or by directly mocking at them. A true artist takes no notice whatever of the public. The public are to him non-existent. He has no poppied or honeyed cakes through which to give the monster sleep or sustenance. He leaves that to the popular novelist. One incomparable novelist we have now in England, Mr George Meredith. There are better artists in France, but France has no one whose view of life is so large, so varied, so imaginatively true. There are tellers of stories in Russia who have a more vivid sense of what pain in fiction may be. But to him belongs philosophy in fiction. His people not merely live, but they live in thought. One can see them from myriad points of view. They are suggestive. There is soul in them and around them. They are interpretative and symbolic. And he who made them, those wonderful quickly-moving figures, made them for his own pleasure, and has never asked the public what they wanted, has never cared to know what they wanted, has never allowed the public to dictate to him or influence him in any way, but has gone on intensifying his own personality, and producing his own individual work. At first none came to him. That did not matter. Then the few came to him. That did not change him. The many have come now. He is still the same. He's an incomparable novelist.

With the decorative arts it is not different. The public clung with really pathetic tenacity to what I believe were the direct traditions of the Great Exhibition of international vulgarity, traditions that were so appalling that the houses in which people lived were only fit for blind people to live in. Beautiful things began to be made, beautiful colours came from the dyer's hand, beautiful patterns from the artist's brain, and the use of beautiful things and their value and importance were set forth. The public were really very indignant. They lost their temper. They said silly things. No one minded. No one was a whit the worse. No one accepted the authority of public opinion. And now it is almost impossible to enter any modern house without seeing some recognition of good taste, some recognition of the value of lovely surroundings, some sign of appreciation of beauty. In fact, people's houses are, as a rule, quite charming nowadays. People have been to a very great extent civilised. It is only fair to state, however, that the extraordinary success of the revolution in house-decoration and furniture and the like has not really been due to the majority of the public developing a very fine taste in such matters. It has been chiefly due to the fact that the craftsmen of things so appreciated the pleasure of making what was beautiful, and woke to such a vivid consciousness of the hideousness and vulgarity of what the public had previously wanted, that they simply starved the public out. It would be quite impossible at the present moment to furnish a room as rooms were furnished a few years ago, without going for everything to an auction of second-hand furniture from some third-rate lodging-house. The things are no longer made. However they may object to it, people must nowadays have something charming in their surroundings. Fortunately for them, their assumption of authority in these art-matters came to entire grief.

It is evident, then, that all authority in such things is bad. People sometimes inquire what form of government is most suitable for an artist to live under. To this question there is only one answer. The form of government that is most suitable to the artist is no government at all. Authority over him and his art is ridiculous. It has been stated that under despotisms artists have produced lovely work. This is not quite so. Artists have visited despots, not as subjects to be tyrannised over, but as wandering wonder-makers, as fascinating vagrant personalities, to be entertained and charmed and suffered to be at peace, and allowed to create. There is this to be said in favour of the despot, that he, being an individual, may have culture, while the mob, being a monster, has none. One who is an Emperor and King may stoop down to pick up a brush for a painter, but when the democracy stoops down it is merely to throw mud. And yet the democracy have not so far to stoop as the emperor. In fact, when they want to throw mud they have not to stoop at all. But there is no necessity to separate the monarch from the mob; all authority is equally bad.

There are three kinds of despots. There is the despot who tyrannises over the body. There is the despot who tyrannises over the soul. There is the despot who tyrannises over the soul and body alike. The first is called the Prince. The second is called the Pope The third is called the People. The Prince may be cultivated. Many Princes have been. Yet in the Prince there is danger. One thinks of Dante at the bitter feast in Verona, of Tasso in Ferrara's madman's cell. It is better for the artist not to live with Princes. The Pope may be cultivated. Many Popes have been; the bad Popes have been. The bad Popes loved Beauty, almost as passionately, nay, with as much passion as the good Popes hated Thought. To the wickedness of the Papacy humanity owes much. The goodness of the Papacy owes a terrible debt to humanity. Yet, though the Vatican has kept the rhetoric of its thunders, and lost the rod of its lightning, it is better for the artist not to live with Popes. It was a Pope who said of Cellini to a conclave of Cardinals that common laws and common authority were not made for men such as he; but it was a Pope who thrust Cellini into prison, and kept him there till he sickened with rage, and created unreal visions for himself, and saw the gilded sun enter his room, and grew so enamoured of it that he sought to escape, and crept out from tower to tower, and falling through dizzy air at dawn, maimed himself, and was by a vine-dresser covered with vine leaves, and carried in a cart to one who, loving beautiful things, had care of him. There is danger in Popes. And as for the People, what of them and their authority? Perhaps of them and their authority one has spoken enough. Their authority is a thing blind, deaf, hideous, grotesque, tragic, amusing, serious, and obscene. It is impossible for the artist to live with the People. All despots bribe. The people bribe and brutalise. Who told them to exercise authority? They were made to live, to listen, and to love. Someone has done them a great wrong. They have marred themselves by imitation of their inferiors. They have taken the sceptre of the Prince. How should they use it? They have taken the triple tiara of the Pope. How should they carry its burden? They are as a clown whose heart is broken. They are as a priest whose soul is not yet born. Let all who love Beauty pity them. Though they themselves love not Beauty, yet let them pity themselves. Who taught them the trick of tyranny?

There are many other things that one might point out. One might point out how the Renaissance was great, because it sought to solve no social problem, and busied itself not about such things, but suffered the individual to develop freely, beautifully, and naturally, and so had great and individual artists, and great and individual men. One might point out how Louis XIV., by creating the modern state, destroyed the individualism of the artist, and made things monstrous in their monotony of repetition, and contemptible in their conformity to rule, and destroyed throughout all France all those fine freedoms of expression that had made tradition new in beauty, and new modes one with antique form. But the past is of no importance. The present is of no importance. It is with the future that we have to deal. For the past is what man should not have been. The present is what man ought not to be. The future is what artists are.

It will, of course, be said that such a scheme as is set forth here is quite unpractical, and goes against human nature. This is perfectly true. It is unpractical, and it goes against human nature. This is why it is worth carrying out, and that is why one proposes it. For what is a practical scheme? A practical scheme is either a scheme that is already in existence, or a scheme that could be carried out under existing conditions. But it is exactly the existing conditions that one objects to; and any scheme that could accept these conditions is wrong and foolish. The conditions will be done away with, and human nature will change. The only thing that one really knows about human nature is that it changes. Change is the one quality we can predicate of it. The systems that fail are those that rely on the permanency of human nature, and not on its growth and development. The error of Louis XIV. was that he thought human nature would always be the same. The result of his error was the French Revolution. It was an admirable result. All the results of the mistakes of governments are quite admirable.

It is to be noted also that Individualism does not come to man with any sickly cant about duty, which merely means doing what other people want because they want it; or any hideous cant about self-sacrifice, which is merely a survival of savage mutilation. In fact, it does not come to man with any claims upon him at all. It comes naturally and inevitably out of man. It is the point to which all development tends. It is the differentiation to which all organisms grow. It is the perfection that is inherent in every mode of life, and towards which every mode of life quickens. And so Individualism exercises no compulsion over man. On the contrary, it says to man that he should suffer no compulsion to be exercised over him. It does not try to force people to be good. It knows that people are good when they are let alone. Man will develop Individualism out of himself. Man is now so developing Individualism. To ask whether Individualism is practical is like asking whether Evolution is practical. Evolution is the law of life, and there is no evolution except towards Individualism. Where this tendency is not expressed, it is a case of artificially-arrested growth, or of disease, or of death.

Individualism will also be unselfish and unaffected. It has been pointed out that one of the results of the extraordinary tyranny of authority is that words are absolutely distorted from their proper and simple meaning, and are used to express the obverse of their right signification. What is true about Art is true about Life. A man is called affected, nowadays, if he dresses as he likes to dress. But in doing that he is acting in a perfectly natural manner. Affectation, in such matters, consists in dressing according to the views of one's neighbour, whose views, as they are the views of the majority, will probably be extremely stupid. Or a man is called selfish if he lives in the manner that seems to him most suitable for the full realisation of his own personality; if, in fact, the primary aim of his life is self-development. But this is the way in which everyone should live. Selfishness is not living as one wishes to live, it is asking others to live as one wishes to live. And unselfishness is letting other people's lives alone, not interfering with them. Selfishness always aims at creating around it an absolute uniformity of type. Unselfishness recognises infinite variety of type as a delightful thing, accepts it, acquiesces in it, enjoys it. It is not selfish to think for oneself. A man who does not think for himself does not think at all. It is grossly selfish to require of one's neighbour that he should think in the same way, and hold the same opinions. Why should he? If he can think, he will probably think differently. If he cannot think, it is monstrous to require thought of any kind from him. A red rose is not selfish because it wants to be a red rose. It would be horribly selfish if it wanted all the other flowers in the garden to be both red and roses. Under Individualism people will be quite natural and absolutely unselfish, and will know the meanings of the words, and realise them in their free, beautiful lives. Nor will men be egotistic as they are now. For the egotist is he who makes claims upon others, and the Individualist will not desire to do that. It will not give him pleasure. When man has realised Individualism, he will also realise sympathy and exercise it freely and spontaneously. Up to the present man has hardly cultivated sympathy at all. He has merely sympathy with pain, and sympathy with pain is not the highest form of sympathy. All sympathy is fine, but sympathy with suffering is the least fine mode. It is tainted with egotism. It is apt to become morbid. There is in it a certain element of terror for our own safety. We become afraid that we ourselves might be as the leper or as the blind, and that no man would have care of us. It is curiously limiting, too. One should sympathise with the entirety of life, not with life's sores and maladies merely, but with life's joy and beauty and energy and health and freedom. The wider sympathy is, of course, the more difficult. It requires more unselfishness. Anybody can sympathise with the sufferings of a friend, but it requires a very fine nature—it requires, in fact, the nature of a true Individualist—to sympathise with a friend's success.

In the modern stress of competition and struggle for place, such sympathy is naturally rare, and is also very much stifled by the immoral ideal of uniformity of type and conformity to rule which is so prevalent everywhere, and is perhaps most obnoxious in England.

Sympathy with pain there will, of course, always be. It is one of the first instincts of man. The animals which are individual, the higher animals, that is to say, share it with us. But it must be remembered that while sympathy with joy intensifies the sum of joy in the world, sympathy with pain does not really diminish the amount of pain. It may make man better able to endure evil, but the evil remains. Sympathy with consumption does not cure consumption; that is what Science does. And when Socialism has solved the problem of poverty, and Science solved the problem of disease, the area of the sentimentalists will be lessened, and the sympathy of man will be large, healthy, and spontaneous. Man will have joy in the contemplation of the joyous life of others.

For it is through joy that the Individualism of the future will develop itself. Christ made no attempt to reconstruct society, and consequently the Individualism that he preached to man could be realised only through pain or in solitude. The ideals that we owe to Christ are the ideals of the man who abandons society entirely, or of the man who resists society absolutely. But man is naturally social. Even the Thebaid became peopled at last. And though the cenobite realises his personality, it is often an impoverished personality that he so realises. Upon the other hand, the terrible truth that pain is a mode through which man may realise himself exercises a wonderful fascination over the world. Shallow speakers and shallow thinkers in pulpits and on platforms often talk about the world's worship of pleasure, and whine against it. But it is rarely in the world's history that its ideal has been one of joy and beauty. The worship of pain has far more often dominated the world. Mediævalism, with its saints and martyrs, its love of self-torture, its wild passion for wounding itself, its gashing with knives, and its whipping with rods—Mediævalism is real Christianity, and the mediæval Christ is the real Christ. When the Renaissance dawned upon the world, and brought with it the new ideals of the beauty of life and the joy of living, men could not understand Christ. Even Art shows us that. The painters of the Renaissance drew Christ as a little boy playing with another boy in a palace or a garden, or lying back in his mother's arms, smiling at her, or at a flower, or at a bright bird; or as a noble, stately figure moving nobly through the world; or as a wonderful figure rising in a sort of ecstasy from death to life. Even when they drew him crucified they drew him as a beautiful God on whom evil men had inflicted suffering. But he did not preoccupy them much. What delighted them was to paint the men and women whom they admired, and to show the loveliness of this lovely earth. They painted many religious pictures—in fact, they painted far too many, and the monotony of type and motive is wearisome, and was bad for art. It was the result of the authority of the public in art-matters, and is to be deplored. But their soul was not in the subject Raphael was a great artist when he painted his portrait of the Pope. When he painted his Madonnas and infant Christs, he is not a great artist at all. Christ had

97

no message for the Renaissance, which was wonderful because it brought an ideal at variance with his, and to find the presentation of the real Christ we must go to mediæval art. There he is one maimed and marred; one who is not comely to look on, because Beauty is a joy; one who is not in fair raiment, because that may be a joy also: he is a beggar who has a marvellous soul; he is a leper whose soul is divine; he needs neither property nor health; he is a God realising his perfection through pain.

The evolution of man is slow. The injustice of men is great. It was necessary that pain should be put forward as a mode of self-realisation. Even now, in some places in the world, the message of Christ is necessary. No one who lived in modern Russia could possibly realise his perfection except by pain. A few Russian artists have realised themselves in Art; in a fiction that is mediæval in character, hecauae its dominant note is the realisation of men through suffering. But for those who are not artists, and to whom there is no mode of life but the actual life of fact, pain is the only door to perfection. A Russian who lives happily under the present system of government in Russia must either believe that man has no soul, or that, if he has, it is not worth developing. A Nihilist who rejects all authority, because he knows authority to be evil, and welcomes all pain, because through that he realises his personality, is a real Christian. To him the Christian ideal is a true thing.

And yet, Christ did not revolt against authority. He accepted the imperial authority of the Roman Empire and paid tribute. He endured the ecclesiastical authority of the Jewish Church, and would not repel its violence by any violence of his own. He had, as I said before, no scheme for the reconstruction of society. But the modern world has schemes. It proposes to do away with poverty and the suffering that it entails. It desires to get rid of pain, and the suffering that pain entails. It trusts to Socialism and to Science as its methods. What it aims at is an Individualism expressing itself through joy. This Individualism will be larger, fuller, lovelier than any Individualism has ever been. Pain is not the ultimate mode of perfection. It is merely provisional and a protest. It has reference to wrong, unhealthy, unjust surroundings. When the wrong, and the disease, and the injustice are removed, it will have no further place. It will have done its work. It was a great

98

work, but it is almost over. Its sphere lessens every day.

Nor will man miss it. For what man has sought for is, indeed, neither pain nor pleasure, but simply Life. Man has sought to live intensely, fully, perfectly. When he can do so without exercising restraint on others, or suffering it ever, and his activities are all pleasurable to him, he will be saner, healthier, more civilised, more himself. Pleasure is Nature's test, her sign of approval. When man is happy, he is in harmony with himself and his environment. The new Individualism, for whose service Socialism, whether it wills it or not, is working, will be perfect harmony. It will be what the Greeks sought for, but could not, except in Thought, realise completely, because they had slaves, and fed them; it will be what the Renaissance sought for, but could not realise completely except in Art, because they had slaves, and starved them. It will be complete, and through it each man will attain to his perfection. The new Individualism is the new Hellenism.

SELECTED POEMS OF OSCAR WILDE INCLUDING THE BALLAD OF READING GAOL

PREFACE

It is thought that a selection from Oscar Wilde's early verses may be of interest to a large public at present familiar only with the always popular *Ballad of Reading Gaol*, also included in this volume. The poems were first collected by their author when he was twenty-sex years old, and though never, until recently, well received by the critics, have survived the test of NINE editions. Readers will be able to make for themselves the obvious and striking contrasts between these first and last phases of Oscar Wilde's literary activity. The intervening period was devoted almost entirely to dramas, prose, fiction, essays, and criticism.

ROBERT ROSS

Reform Club,

April 5, 1911.

NOTE

At the end of the complete text will be found a shorter version based on the original draft of the poem. This is included for the benefit of reciters and their audiences who have found the entire poem too long for declamation. I have tried to obviate a difficulty, without officiously exercising the ungrateful prerogatives of a literary executor, by falling back on a text which represents the author's first scheme for a poem—never intended of course for recitation.

ROBERT ROSS

IN MEMORIAM

C. T. W.

Sometimes trooper of

The Royal Horse Guards

Obiit H.M. Prison

Reading, Berkshire

July 7th, 1896

THE BALLAD OF READING GAOL

I

He did not wear his scarlet coat,
  For blood and wine are red,
And blood and wine were on his hands
  When they found him with the dead,
The poor dead woman whom he loved,
  And murdered in her bed.

He walked amongst the Trial Men
  In a suit of shabby grey;
A cricket cap was on his head,
  And his step seemed light and gay;
But I never saw a man who looked
  So wistfully at the day.

I never saw a man who looked
  With such a wistful eye
Upon that little tent of blue
  Which prisoners call the sky,
And at every drifting cloud that went

With sails of silver by.

I walked, with other souls in pain,

Within another ring,

And was wondering if the man had done

A great or little thing,

When a voice behind me whispered low,

'That fellow's got to swing.'

Dear Christ! the very prison walls

Suddenly seemed to reel,

And the sky above my head became

Like a casque of scorching steel;

And, though I was a soul in pain,

My pain I could not feel.

I only knew what hunted thought

Quickened his step, and why

He looked upon the garish day

With such a wistful eye;

The man had killed the thing he loved,

And so he had to die.

Yet each man kills the thing he loves,

By each let this be heard,

Some do it with a bitter look,

Some with a flattering word,

The coward does it with a kiss,

The brave man with a sword!

Some kill their love when they are young,

And some when they are old;

Some strangle with the hands of Lust,

Some with the hands of Gold:

The kindest use a knife, because

The dead so soon grow cold.

Some love too little, some too long,

Some sell, and others buy;

Some do the deed with many tears,

And some without a sigh:

For each man kills the thing he loves,

Yet each man does not die.

He does not die a death of shame

On a day of dark disgrace,

Nor have a noose about his neck,

Nor a cloth upon his face,

Nor drop feet foremost through the floor

Into an empty space.

He does not sit with silent men

Who watch him night and day;

Who watch him when he tries to weep,

And when he tries to pray;

Who watch him lest himself should rob

The prison of its prey.

He does not wake at dawn to see

Dread figures throng his room,

The shivering Chaplain robed in white,

The Sheriff stern with gloom,

And the Governor all in shiny black,

With the yellow face of Doom.

He does not rise in piteous haste

To put on convict-clothes,

While some coarse-mouthed Doctor gloats, and notes

Each new and nerve-twitched pose,

Fingering a watch whose little ticks

Are like horrible hammer-blows.

He does not know that sickening thirst
 That sands one's throat, before
The hangman with his gardener's gloves
 Slips through the padded door,
And binds one with three leathern thongs,
 That the throat may thirst no more.

He does not bend his head to hear
 The Burial Office read,
Nor, while the terror of his soul
 Tells him he is not dead,
Cross his own coffin, as he moves
 Into the hideous shed.

He does not stare upon the air
 Through a little roof of glass:
He does not pray with lips of clay
 For his agony to pass;
Nor feel upon his shuddering cheek
 The kiss of Caiaphas.

II

Six weeks our guardsman walked the yard,

In the suit of shabby grey:

His cricket cap was on his head,

   And his step seemed light and gay,

But I never saw a man who looked

   So wistfully at the day.

I never saw a man who looked

   With such a wistful eye

Upon that little tent of blue

   Which prisoners call the sky,

And at every wandering cloud that trailed

   Its ravelled fleeces by.

He did not wring his hands, as do

   Those witless men who dare

To try to rear the changeling Hope

   In the cave of black Despair:

He only looked upon the sun,

   And drank the morning air.

He did not wring his hands nor weep,

   Nor did he peek or pine,

But he drank the air as though it held

Some healthful anodyne;
With open mouth he drank the sun
As though it had been wine!

And I and all the souls in pain,
Who tramped the other ring,
Forgot if we ourselves had done
A great or little thing,
And watched with gaze of dull amaze
The man who had to swing.

And strange it was to see him pass
With a step so light and gay,
And strange it was to see him look
So wistfully at the day,
And strange it was to think that he
Had such a debt to pay.

For oak and elm have pleasant leaves
That in the springtime shoot:
But grim to see is the gallows-tree,
With its adder-bitten root,
And, green or dry, a man must die

Before it bears its fruit!

The loftiest place is that seat of grace
   For which all worldlings try:
But who would stand in hempen band
   Upon a scaffold high,
And through a murderer's collar take
   His last look at the sky?

It is sweet to dance to violins
   When Love and Life are fair:
To dance to flutes, to dance to lutes
   Is delicate and rare:
But it is not sweet with nimble feet
   To dance upon the air!

So with curious eyes and sick surmise
   We watched him day by day,
And wondered if each one of us
   Would end the self-same way,
For none can tell to what red Hell
   His sightless soul may stray.

At last the dead man walked no more

Amongst the Trial Men,

And I knew that he was standing up

In the black dock's dreadful pen,

And that never would I see his face

In God's sweet world again.

Like two doomed ships that pass in storm

We had crossed each other's way:

But we made no sign, we said no word,

We had no word to say;

For we did not meet in the holy night,

But in the shameful day.

A prison wall was round us both,

Two outcast men we were:

The world had thrust us from its heart,

And God from out His care:

And the iron gin that waits for Sin

Had caught us in its snare.

III

In Debtors' Yard the stones are hard,

And the dripping wall is high,

So it was there he took the air

   Beneath the leaden sky,

And by each side a Warder walked,

   For fear the man might die.

Or else he sat with those who watched

   His anguish night and day;

Who watched him when he rose to weep,

   And when he crouched to pray;

Who watched him lest himself should rob

   Their scaffold of its prey.

The Governor was strong upon

   The Regulations Act:

The Doctor said that Death was but

   A scientific fact:

And twice a day the Chaplain called,

   And left a little tract.

And twice a day he smoked his pipe,

   And drank his quart of beer:

His soul was resolute, and held

   No hiding-place for fear;

He often said that he was glad

    The hangman's hands were near.

But why he said so strange a thing

    No Warder dared to ask:

For he to whom a watcher's doom

    Is given as his task,

Must set a lock upon his lips,

    And make his face a mask.

Or else he might be moved, and try

    To comfort or console:

And what should Human Pity do

    Pent up in Murderers' Hole?

What word of grace in such a place

    Could help a brother's soul?

With slouch and swing around the ring

    We trod the Fools' Parade!

We did not care: we knew we were

    The Devil's Own Brigade:

And shaven head and feet of lead

    Make a merry masquerade.

We tore the tarry rope to shreds

With blunt and bleeding nails;

We rubbed the doors, and scrubbed the floors,

And cleaned the shining rails:

And, rank by rank, we soaped the plank,

And clattered with the pails.

We sewed the sacks, we broke the stones,

We turned the dusty drill:

We banged the tins, and bawled the hymns,

And sweated on the mill:

But in the heart of every man

Terror was lying still.

So still it lay that every day

Crawled like a weed-clogged wave:

And we forgot the bitter lot

That waits for fool and knave,

Till once, as we tramped in from work,

We passed an open grave.

With yawning mouth the yellow hole

Gaped for a living thing;

The very mud cried out for blood

To the thirsty asphalte ring:

And we knew that ere one dawn grew fair

Some prisoner had to swing.

Right in we went, with soul intent

On Death and Dread and Doom:

The hangman, with his little bag,

Went shuffling through the gloom:

And each man trembled as he crept

Into his numbered tomb.

That night the empty corridors

Were full of forms of Fear,

And up and down the iron town

Stole feet we could not hear,

And through the bars that hide the stars

White faces seemed to peer.

He lay as one who lies and dreams

In a pleasant meadow-land,

The watchers watched him as he slept,

And could not understand

How one could sleep so sweet a sleep

  With a hangman close at hand.

But there is no sleep when men must weep

  Who never yet have wept:

So we—the fool, the fraud, the knave—

  That endless vigil kept,

And through each brain on hands of pain

  Another's terror crept.

Alas! it is a fearful thing

  To feel another's guilt!

For, right within, the sword of Sin

  Pierced to its poisoned hilt,

And as molten lead were the tears we shed

  For the blood we had not spilt.

The Warders with their shoes of felt

  Crept by each padlocked door,

And peeped and saw, with eyes of awe,

  Grey figures on the floor,

And wondered why men knelt to pray

Who never prayed before.

All through the night we knelt and prayed,
  Mad mourners of a corse!
The troubled plumes of midnight were
  The plumes upon a hearse:
And bitter wine upon a sponge
  Was the savour of Remorse.

The grey cock crew, the red cock crew,
  But never came the day:
And crooked shapes of Terror crouched,
  In the corners where we lay:
And each evil sprite that walks by night
  Before us seemed to play.

They glided past, they glided fast,
  Like travellers through a mist:
They mocked the moon in a rigadoon
  Of delicate turn and twist,
And with formal pace and loathsome grace
  The phantoms kept their tryst.

With mop and mow, we saw them go,

Slim shadows hand in hand:

About, about, in ghostly rout

They trod a saraband:

And the damned grotesques made arabesques,

Like the wind upon the sand!

With the pirouettes of marionettes,

They tripped on pointed tread:

But with flutes of Fear they filled the ear,

As their grisly masque they led,

And loud they sang, and long they sang,

For they sang to wake the dead.

'Oho!' they cried, 'The world is wide,

But fettered limbs go lame!

And once, or twice, to throw the dice

Is a gentlemanly game,

But he does not win who plays with Sin

In the secret House of Shame.'

No things of air these antics were,

That frolicked with such glee:

To men whose lives were held in gyves,

And whose feet might not go free,

Ah! wounds of Christ! they were living things,

Most terrible to see.

Around, around, they waltzed and wound;

Some wheeled in smirking pairs;

With the mincing step of a demirep

Some sidled up the stairs:

And with subtle sneer, and fawning leer,

Each helped us at our prayers.

The morning wind began to moan,

But still the night went on:

Through its giant loom the web of gloom

Crept till each thread was spun:

And, as we prayed, we grew afraid

Of the Justice of the Sun.

The moaning wind went wandering round

The weeping prison-wall:

Till like a wheel of turning steel

We felt the minutes crawl:

O moaning wind! what had we done

To have such a seneschal?

At last I saw the shadowed bars,

Like a lattice wrought in lead,

Move right across the whitewashed wall

That faced my three-plank bed,

And I knew that somewhere in the world

God's dreadful dawn was red.

At six o'clock we cleaned our cells,

At seven all was still,

But the sough and swing of a mighty wing

The prison seemed to fill,

For the Lord of Death with icy breath

Had entered in to kill.

He did not pass in purple pomp,

Nor ride a moon-white steed.

Three yards of cord and a sliding board

Are all the gallows' need:

So with rope of shame the Herald came

To do the secret deed.

We were as men who through a fen

Of filthy darkness grope:

We did not dare to breathe a prayer,

   Or to give our anguish scope:

Something was dead in each of us,

   And what was dead was Hope.

For Man's grim Justice goes its way,

   And will not swerve aside:

It slays the weak, it slays the strong,

   It has a deadly stride:

With iron heel it slays the strong,

   The monstrous parricide!

We waited for the stroke of eight:

   Each tongue was thick with thirst:

For the stroke of eight is the stroke of Fate

   That makes a man accursed,

And Fate will use a running noose

   For the best man and the worst.

We had no other thing to do,

   Save to wait for the sign to come:

So, like things of stone in a valley lone,

Quiet we sat and dumb:

But each man's heart beat thick and quick,

Like a madman on a drum!

With sudden shock the prison-clock

Smote on the shivering air,

And from all the gaol rose up a wail

Of impotent despair,

Like the sound that frightened marshes hear

From some leper in his lair.

And as one sees most fearful things

In the crystal of a dream,

We saw the greasy hempen rope

Hooked to the blackened beam,

And heard the prayer the hangman's snare

Strangled into a scream.

And all the woe that moved him so

That he gave that bitter cry,

And the wild regrets, and the bloody sweats,

None knew so well as I:

For he who lives more lives than one

More deaths than one must die.

<u>IV</u>

There is no chapel on the day
  On which they hang a man:
The Chaplain's heart is far too sick,
  Or his face is far too wan,
Or there is that written in his eyes
  Which none should look upon.

So they kept us close till nigh on noon,
  And then they rang the bell,
And the Warders with their jingling keys
  Opened each listening cell,
And down the iron stair we tramped,
  Each from his separate Hell.

Out into God's sweet air we went,
  But not in wonted way,
For this man's face was white with fear,
  And that man's face was grey,
And I never saw sad men who looked
  So wistfully at the day.

I never saw sad men who looked

    With such a wistful eye

Upon that little tent of blue

    We prisoners called the sky,

And at every careless cloud that passed

    In happy freedom by.

But there were those amongst us all

    Who walked with downcast head,

And knew that, had each got his due,

    They should have died instead:

He had but killed a thing that lived,

    Whilst they had killed the dead.

For he who sins a second time

    Wakes a dead soul to pain,

And draws it from its spotted shroud,

    And makes it bleed again,

And makes it bleed great gouts of blood,

    And makes it bleed in vain!

    Like ape or clown, in monstrous garb

With crooked arrows starred,

Silently we went round and round

The slippery asphalte yard;

Silently we went round and round,

And no man spoke a word.

Silently we went round and round,

And through each hollow mind

The Memory of dreadful things

Rushed like a dreadful wind,

And Horror stalked before each man,

And Terror crept behind.

The Warders strutted up and down,

And kept their herd of brutes,

Their uniforms were spick and span,

And they wore their Sunday suits,

But we knew the work they had been at,

By the quicklime on their boots.

For where a grave had opened wide,

There was no grave at all:

Only a stretch of mud and sand

By the hideous prison-wall,

And a little heap of burning lime,

That the man should have his pall.

For he has a pall, this wretched man,

Such as few men can claim:

Deep down below a prison-yard,

Naked for greater shame,

He lies, with fetters on each foot,

Wrapt in a sheet of flame!

And all the while the burning lime

Eats flesh and bone away,

It eats the brittle bone by night,

And the soft flesh by day,

It eats the flesh and bone by turns,

But it eats the heart alway.

For three long years they will not sow

Or root or seedling there:

For three long years the unblessed spot

Will sterile be and bare,

And look upon the wondering sky

With unreproachful stare.

They think a murderer's heart would taint
   Each simple seed they sow.
It is not true! God's kindly earth
   Is kindlier than men know,
And the red rose would but blow more red,
   The white rose whiter blow.

Out of his mouth a red, red rose!
   Out of his heart a white!
For who can say by what strange way,
   Christ brings His will to light,
Since the barren staff the pilgrim bore
   Bloomed in the great Pope's sight?

But neither milk-white rose nor red
   May bloom in prison-air;
The shard, the pebble, and the flint,
   Are what they give us there:
For flowers have been known to heal
   A common man's despair.

So never will wine-red rose or white,

Petal by petal, fall

On that stretch of mud and sand that lies

By the hideous prison-wall,

To tell the men who tramp the yard

That God's Son died for all.

Yet though the hideous prison-wall

Still hems him round and round,

And a spirit may not walk by night

That is with fetters bound,

And a spirit may but weep that lies

In such unholy ground,

He is at peace—this wretched man—

At peace, or will be soon:

There is no thing to make him mad,

Nor does Terror walk at noon,

For the lampless Earth in which he lies

Has neither Sun nor Moon.

They hanged him as a beast is hanged:

They did not even toll

A requiem that might have brought

Rest to his startled soul,

But hurriedly they took him out,

And hid him in a hole.

They stripped him of his canvas clothes,

And gave him to the flies:

They mocked the swollen purple throat,

And the stark and staring eyes:

And with laughter loud they heaped the shroud

In which their convict lies.

The Chaplain would not kneel to pray

By his dishonoured grave:

Nor mark it with that blessed Cross

That Christ for sinners gave,

Because the man was one of those

Whom Christ came down to save.

Yet all is well; he has but passed

To Life's appointed bourne:

And alien tears will fill for him

Pity's long-broken urn,

For his mourners will be outcast men,

And outcasts always mourn

V

I know not whether Laws be right,
 Or whether Laws be wrong;
All that we know who lie in gaol
 Is that the wall is strong;
And that each day is like a year,
 A year whose days are long.

But this I know, that every Law
 That men have made for Man,
Since first Man took his brother's life,
 And the sad world began,
But straws the wheat and saves the chaff
 With a most evil fan.

This too I know—and wise it were
 If each could know the same—
That every prison that men build
 Is built with bricks of shame,
And bound with bars lest Christ should see
 How men their brothers maim.

With bars they blur the gracious moon,
  And blind the goodly sun:
And they do well to hide their Hell,
  For in it things are done
That Son of God nor son of Man
  Ever should look upon!

The vilest deeds like poison weeds,
  Bloom well in prison-air;
It is only what is good in Man
  That wastes and withers there:
Pale Anguish keeps the heavy gate,
  And the Warder is Despair.

For they starve the little frightened child
  Till it weeps both night and day:
And they scourge the weak, and flog the fool,
  And gibe the old and grey,
And some grow mad, and all grow bad,
  And none a word may say.

Each narrow cell in which we dwell

Is a foul and dark latrine,

And the fetid breath of living Death

Chokes up each grated screen,

And all, but Lust, is turned to dust

In Humanity's machine.

The brackish water that we drink

Creeps with a loathsome slime,

And the bitter bread they weigh in scales

Is full of chalk and lime,

And Sleep will not lie down, but walks

Wild-eyed, and cries to Time.

But though lean Hunger and green Thirst

Like asp with adder fight,

We have little care of prison fare,

For what chills and kills outright

Is that every stone one lifts by day

Becomes one's heart by night.

With midnight always in one's heart,

And twilight in one's cell,

We turn the crank, or tear the rope,

Each in his separate Hell,

And the silence is more awful far

Than the sound of a brazen bell.

And never a human voice comes near

To speak a gentle word:

And the eye that watches through the door

Is pitiless and hard:

And by all forgot, we rot and rot,

With soul and body marred.

And thus we rust Life's iron chain

Degraded and alone:

And some men curse, and some men weep,

And some men make no moan:

But God's eternal Laws are kind

And break the heart of stone.

And every human heart that breaks,

In prison-cell or yard,

Is as that broken box that gave

Its treasure to the Lord,

And filled the unclean leper's house

With the scent of costliest nard.

Ah! happy they whose hearts can break
    And peace of pardon win!
How else may man make straight his plan
    And cleanse his soul from Sin?
How else but through a broken heart
    May Lord Christ enter in?

And he of the swollen purple throat,
    And the stark and staring eyes,
Waits for the holy hands that took
    The Thief to Paradise;
And a broken and a contrite heart
    The Lord will not despise.

The man in red who reads the Law
    Gave him three weeks of life,
Three little weeks in which to heal
    His soul of his soul's strife,
And cleanse from every blot of blood
    The hand that held the knife.

And with tears of blood he cleansed the hand,

The hand that held the steel:

For only blood can wipe out blood,

And only tears can heal:

And the crimson stain that was of Cain

Became Christ's snow-white seal.

VI

In Reading gaol by Reading town

There is a pit of shame,

And in it lies a wretched man

Eaten by teeth of flame,

In a burning winding-sheet he lies,

And his grave has got no name.

And there, till Christ call forth the dead,

In silence let him lie:

No need to waste the foolish tear,

Or heave the windy sigh:

The man had killed the thing he loved,

And so he had to die.

And all men kill the thing they love,

By all let this be heard,

Some do it with a bitter look,

Some with a flattering word,

The coward does it with a kiss,

The brave man with a sword!

APPENDIX THE BALLAD OF READING GAOL

A VERSION BASED ON THE ORIGINAL DRAFT OF THE POEM

I

He did not wear his scarlet coat,

    For blood and wine are red,

And blood and wine were on his hands

    When they found him with the dead,

The poor dead woman whom he loved,

    And murdered in her bed.

He walked amongst the Trial Men

    In a suit of shabby grey;

A cricket cap was on his head,

    And his step seemed light and gay;

But I never saw a man who looked

    So wistfully at the day.

I never saw a man who looked

    With such a wistful eye

Upon that little tent of blue

    Which prisoners call the sky,

And at every drifting cloud that went

  With sails of silver by.

I walked, with other souls in pain,

  Within another ring,

And was wondering if the man had done

  A great or little thing,

When a voice behind me whispered low,

  'That fellow's got to swing.'

Dear Christ! the very prison walls

  Suddenly seemed to reel,

And the sky above my head became

  Like a casque of scorching steel;

And, though I was a soul in pain,

  My pain I could not feel.

I only knew what hunted thought

  Quickened his step, and why

He looked upon the garish day

  With such a wistful eye;

The man had killed the thing he loved,

  And so he had to die.

144

Yet each man kills the thing he loves,
By each let this be heard,
Some do it with a bitter look,
Some with a flattering word,
The coward does it with a kiss,
The brave man with a sword!

Some kill their love when they are young,
And some when they are old;
Some strangle with the hands of Lust,
Some with the hands of Gold:
The kindest use a knife, because
The dead so soon grow cold.

Some love too little, some too long,
Some sell, and others buy;
Some do the deed with many tears,
And some without a sigh:
For each man kills the thing he loves,
Yet each man does not die.

He does not die a death of shame

On a day of dark disgrace,
Nor have a noose about his neck,
Nor a cloth upon his face,
Nor drop feet foremost through the floor
Into an empty space.

He does not wake at dawn to see
Dread figures throng his room,
The shivering Chaplain robed in white,
The Sheriff stern with gloom,
And the Governor all in shiny black,
With the yellow face of Doom.

He does not rise in piteous haste
To put on convict-clothes,
While some coarse-mouthed Doctor gloats, and notes
Each new and nerve-twitched pose,
Fingering a watch whose little ticks
Are like horrible hammer-blows.

He does not know that sickening thirst
That sands one's throat, before
The hangman with his gardener's gloves

Slips through the padded door,

And binds one with three leathern thongs,

That the throat may thirst no more.

He does not bend his head to hear

The Burial Office read,

Nor, while the terror of his soul

Tells him he is not dead,

Cross his own coffin, as he moves

Into the hideous shed.

He does not stare upon the air

Through a little roof of glass:

He does not pray with lips of clay

For his agony to pass;

Nor feel upon his shuddering cheek

The kiss of Caiaphas.

II

Six weeks our guardsman walked the yard,

In the suit of shabby grey:

His cricket cap was on his head,

And his step seemed light and gay,

But I never saw a man who looked

147

So wistfully at the day.

He did not wring his hands nor weep,

   Nor did he peek or pine,

But he drank the air as though it held

   Some healthful anodyne;

With open mouth he drank the sun

   As though it had been wine!

And I and all the souls in pain,

   Who tramped the other ring,

Forgot if we ourselves had done

   A great or little thing,

And watched with gaze of dull amaze

   The man who had to swing.

So with curious eyes and sick surmise

   We watched him day by day,

And wondered if each one of us

   Would end the self-same way,

For none can tell to what red Hell

   His sightless soul may stray.

At last the dead man walked no more

Amongst the Trial Men,

And I knew that he was standing up

In the black dock's dreadful pen,

And that never would I see his face

In God's sweet world again.

Like two doomed ships that pass in storm

We had crossed each other's way:

But we made no sign, we said no word,

We had no word to say;

For we did not meet in the holy night,

But in the shameful day.

A prison wall was round us both,

Two outcast men we were:

The world had thrust us from its heart,

And God from out His care:

And the iron gin that waits for Sin

Had caught us in its snare.

III

In Debtors' Yard the stones are hard,

And the dripping wall is high,

So it was there he took the air

   Beneath the leaden sky,

And by each side a Warder walked,

   For fear the man might die.

Or else he sat with those who watched

   His anguish night and day;

Who watched him when he rose to weep,

   And when he crouched to pray;

Who watched him lest himself should rob

   Their scaffold of its prey.

And twice a day he smoked his pipe,

   And drank his quart of beer:

His soul was resolute, and held

   No hiding-place for fear;

He often said that he was glad

   The hangman's hands were near.

But why he said so strange a thing

   No Warder dared to ask:

For he to whom a watcher's doom

   Is given as his task,

Must set a lock upon his lips,

    And make his face a mask.

With slouch and swing around the ring

    We trod the Fools' Parade!

We did not care: we knew we were

    The Devil's Own Brigade:

And shaven head and feet of lead

    Make a merry masquerade.

We tore the tarry rope to shreds

    With blunt and bleeding nails;

We rubbed the doors, and scrubbed the floors,

    And cleaned the shining rails:

And, rank by rank, we soaped the plank,

    And clattered with the pails.

We sewed the sacks, we broke the stones,

    We turned the dusty drill:

We banged the tins, and bawled the hymns,

    And sweated on the mill:

But in the heart of every man

    Terror was lying still.

So still it lay that every day

   Crawled like a weed-clogged wave:

And we forgot the bitter lot

   That waits for fool and knave,

Till once, as we tramped in from work,

   We passed an open grave.

Right in we went, with soul intent

   On Death and Dread and Doom:

The hangman, with his little bag,

   Went shuffling through the gloom:

And each man trembled as he crept

   Into his numbered tomb.

That night the empty corridors

   Were full of forms of Fear,

And up and down the iron town

   Stole feet we could not hear,

And through the bars that hide the stars

   White faces seemed to peer.

But there is no sleep when men must weep

Who never yet have wept:
So we—the fool, the fraud, the knave—
   That endless vigil kept,
And through each brain on hands of pain
   Another's terror crept.

Alas! it is a fearful thing
   To feel another's guilt!
For, right within, the sword of Sin
   Pierced to its poisoned hilt,
And as molten lead were the tears we shed
   For the blood we had not spilt.

The Warders with their shoes of felt
   Crept by each padlocked door,
And peeped and saw, with eyes of awe,
   Grey figures on the floor,
And wondered why men knelt to pray
   Who never prayed before.

The morning wind began to moan,
   But still the night went on:
Through its giant loom the web of gloom

Crept till each thread was spun:

And, as we prayed, we grew afraid

Of the Justice of the Sun.

At last I saw the shadowed bars,

Like a lattice wrought in lead,

Move right across the whitewashed wall

That faced my three-plank bed,

And I knew that somewhere in the world

God's dreadful dawn was red.

At six o'clock we cleaned our cells,

At seven all was still,

But the sough and swing of a mighty wing

The prison seemed to fill,

For the Lord of Death with icy breath

Had entered in to kill.

He did not pass in purple pomp,

Nor ride a moon-white steed.

Three yards of cord and a sliding board

Are all the gallows' need:

So with rope of shame the Herald came

To do the secret deed.

We waited for the stroke of eight:
    Each tongue was thick with thirst:
For the stroke of eight is the stroke of Fate
    That makes a man accursed,
And Fate will use a running noose
    For the best man and the worst.

We had no other thing to do,
    Save to wait for the sign to come:
So, like things of stone in a valley lone,
    Quiet we sat and dumb:
But each man's heart beat thick and quick,
    Like a madman on a drum!

With sudden shock the prison-clock
    Smote on the shivering air,
And from all the gaol rose up a wail
    Of impotent despair,
Like the sound that frightened marshes hear
    From some leper in his lair.

And as one sees most fearful things

In the crystal of a dream,

We saw the greasy hempen rope

Hooked to the blackened beam,

And heard the prayer the hangman's snare

Strangled into a scream.

And all the woe that moved him so

That he gave that bitter cry,

And the wild regrets, and the bloody sweats,

None knew so well as I:

For he who lives more lives than one

More deaths than one must die.

IV

There is no chapel on the day

On which they hang a man:

The Chaplain's heart is far too sick,

Or his face is far too wan,

Or there is that written in his eyes

Which none should look upon.

So they kept us close till nigh on noon,

And then they rang the bell,

And the Warders with their jingling keys
    Opened each listening cell,
And down the iron stair we tramped,
    Each from his separate Hell.

Out into God's sweet air we went,
    But not in wonted way,
For this man's face was white with fear,
    And that man's face was grey,
And I never saw sad men who looked
    So wistfully at the day.

I never saw sad men who looked
    With such a wistful eye
Upon that little tent of blue
    We prisoners called the sky,
And at every careless cloud that passed
    In happy freedom by.

But there were those amongst us all
    Who walked with downcast head,
And knew that, had each got his due,
    They should have died instead:

He had but killed a thing that lived,

    Whilst they had killed the dead.

For he who sins a second time

    Wakes a dead soul to pain,

And draws it from its spotted shroud,

    And makes it bleed again,

And makes it bleed great gouts of blood,

    And makes it bleed in vain!

Like ape or clown, in monstrous garb

    With crooked arrows starred,

Silently we went round and round

    The slippery asphalte yard;

Silently we went round and round,

    And no man spoke a word.

Silently we went round and round,

    And through each hollow mind

The Memory of dreadful things

    Rushed like a dreadful wind,

And Horror stalked before each man,

    And Terror crept behind.

The Warders strutted up and down,

    And kept their herd of brutes,

Their uniforms were spick and span,

    And they wore their Sunday suits,

But we knew the work they had been at,

    By the quicklime on their boots.

For where a grave had opened wide,

    There was no grave at all:

Only a stretch of mud and sand

    By the hideous prison-wall,

And a little heap of burning lime,

    That the man should have his pall.

For he has a pall, this wretched man,

    Such as few men can claim:

Deep down below a prison-yard,

    Naked for greater shame,

He lies, with fetters on each foot,

    Wrapt in a sheet of flame!

For three long years they will not sow

Or root or seedling there:

For three long years the unblessed spot

    Will sterile be and bare,

And look upon the wondering sky

    With unreproachful stare.

They think a murderer's heart would taint

    Each simple seed they sow.

It is not true! God's kindly earth

    Is kindlier than men know,

And the red rose would but blow more red,

    The white rose whiter blow.

Out of his mouth a red, red rose!

    Out of his heart a white!

For who can say by what strange way,

    Christ brings His will to light,

Since the barren staff the pilgrim bore

    Bloomed in the great Pope's sight?

But neither milk-white rose nor red

    May bloom in prison-air;

The shard, the pebble, and the flint,

Are what they give us there:

For flowers have been known to heal

A common man's despair.

So never will wine-red rose or white,

Petal by petal, fall

On that stretch of mud and sand that lies

By the hideous prison-wall,

To tell the men who tramp the yard

That God's Son died for all.

He is at peace—this wretched man—

At peace, or will be soon:

There is no thing to make him mad,

Nor does Terror walk at noon,

For the lampless Earth in which he lies

Has neither Sun nor Moon.

The Chaplain would not kneel to pray

By his dishonoured grave:

Nor mark it with that blessed Cross

That Christ for sinners gave,

Because the man was one of those

Whom Christ came down to save.

Yet all is well; he has but passed
   To Life's appointed bourne:
And alien tears will fill for him
   Pity's long-broken urn,
For his mourners will be outcast men,
   And outcasts always mourn.

POEMS

AVE IMPERATRIX

Set in this stormy Northern sea,

    Queen of these restless fields of tide,

England! what shall men say of thee,

    Before whose feet the worlds divide?

The earth, a brittle globe of glass,

    Lies in the hollow of thy hand,

And through its heart of crystal pass,

    Like shadows through a twilight land,

The spears of crimson-suited war,

    The long white-crested waves of fight,

And all the deadly fires which are

    The torches of the lords of Night.

The yellow leopards, strained and lean,

    The treacherous Russian knows so well,

With gaping blackened jaws are seen

Leap through the hail of screaming shell.

The strong sea-lion of England's wars

Hath left his sapphire cave of sea,

To battle with the storm that mars

The stars of England's chivalry.

The brazen-throated clarion blows

Across the Pathan's reedy fen,

And the high steeps of Indian snows

Shake to the tread of armèd men.

And many an Afghan chief, who lies

Beneath his cool pomegranate-trees,

Clutches his sword in fierce surmise

When on the mountain-side he sees

The fleet-foot Marri scout, who comes

To tell how he hath heard afar

The measured roll of English drums

Beat at the gates of Kandahar.

For southern wind and east wind meet

Where, girt and crowned by sword and fire,

England with bare and bloody feet

Climbs the steep road of wide empire.

O lonely Himalayan height,

Grey pillar of the Indian sky,

Where saw'st thou last in clanging flight

Our wingèd dogs of Victory?

The almond-groves of Samarcand,

Bokhara, where red lilies blow,

And Oxus, by whose yellow sand

The grave white-turbaned merchants go:

And on from thence to Ispahan,

The gilded garden of the sun,

Whence the long dusty caravan

Brings cedar wood and vermilion;

And that dread city of Cabool

Set at the mountain's scarpèd feet,

Whose marble tanks are ever full

With water for the noonday heat:

Where through the narrow straight Bazaar

  A little maid Circassian

Is led, a present from the Czar

  Unto some old and bearded Khan,—

Here have our wild war-eagles flown,

  And flapped wide wings in fiery fight;

But the sad dove, that sits alone

  In England—she hath no delight.

In vain the laughing girl will lean

  To greet her love with love-lit eyes:

Down in some treacherous black ravine,

  Clutching his flag, the dead boy lies.

And many a moon and sun will see

  The lingering wistful children wait

To climb upon their father's knee;

  And in each house made desolate

Pale women who have lost their lord

  Will kiss the relics of the slain—

Some tarnished epaulette—some sword—

    Poor toys to soothe such anguished pain.

For not in quiet English fields

    Are these, our brothers, lain to rest,

Where we might deck their broken shields

    With all the flowers the dead love best.

For some are by the Delhi walls,

    And many in the Afghan land,

And many where the Ganges falls

    Through seven mouths of shifting sand.

And some in Russian waters lie,

    And others in the seas which are

The portals to the East, or by

    The wind-swept heights of Trafalgar.

O wandering graves! O restless sleep!

    O silence of the sunless day!

O still ravine! O stormy deep!

    Give up your prey! Give up your prey!

And thou whose wounds are never healed,

Whose weary race is never won,

O Cromwell's England! must thou yield

For every inch of ground a son?

Go! crown with thorns thy gold-crowned head,

Change thy glad song to song of pain;

Wind and wild wave have got thy dead,

And will not yield them back again.

Wave and wild wind and foreign shore

Possess the flower of English land—

Lips that thy lips shall kiss no more,

Hands that shall never clasp thy hand.

What profit now that we have bound

The whole round world with nets of gold,

If hidden in our heart is found

The care that groweth never old?

What profit that our galleys ride,

Pine-forest-like, on every main?

Ruin and wreck are at our side,

Grim warders of the House of Pain.

Where are the brave, the strong, the fleet?
  Where is our English chivalry?
Wild grasses are their burial-sheet,
  And sobbing waves their threnody.

O loved ones lying far away,
  What word of love can dead lips send!
O wasted dust! O senseless clay!
  Is this the end! is this the end!

Peace, peace! we wrong the noble dead
  To vex their solemn slumber so;
Though childless, and with thorn-crowned head,
  Up the steep road must England go,

Yet when this fiery web is spun,
  Her watchmen shall descry from far
The young Republic like a sun
  Rise from these crimson seas of war.

TO MY WIFE
WITH A COPY OF MY POEMS

I can write no stately proem

    As a prelude to my lay;

From a poet to a poem

    I would dare to say.

For if of these fallen petals

    One to you seem fair,

Love will waft it till it settles

    On your hair.

And when wind and winter harden

    All the loveless land,

It will whisper of the garden,

    You will understand.

MAGDALEN WALKS

[After gaining the Berkeley Gold Medal for Greek at Trinity College, Dublin, in 1874, Oscar Wilde proceeded to Oxford, where he obtained a demyship at Magdalen College. He is the only real poet on the books of that institution.]

The little white clouds are racing over the sky,
  And the fields are strewn with the gold of the flower of March,
  The daffodil breaks under foot, and the tasselled larch
Sways and swings as the thrush goes hurrying by.

A delicate odour is borne on the wings of the morning breeze,
  The odour of deep wet grass, and of brown new-furrowed earth,
  The birds are singing for joy of the Spring's glad birth,
Hopping from branch to branch on the rocking trees.

And all the woods are alive with the murmur and sound of Spring,
  And the rose-bud breaks into pink on the climbing briar,
  And the crocus-bed is a quivering moon of fire
Girdled round with the belt of an amethyst ring.

And the plane to the pine-tree is whispering some tale of love
  Till it rustles with laughter and tosses its mantle of green,

And the gloom of the wych-elm's hollow is lit with the iris sheen

Of the burnished rainbow throat and the silver breast of a dove.

See! the lark starts up from his bed in the meadow there,

    Breaking the gossamer threads and the nets of dew,

    And flashing adown the river, a flame of blue!

The kingfisher flies like an arrow, and wounds the air.

THEOCRITUS

A VILLANELLE

O singer of Persephone!
  In the dim meadows desolate
Dost thou remember Sicily?

Still through the ivy flits the bee
  Where Amaryllis lies in state;
O Singer of Persephone!

Simætha calls on Hecate
  And hears the wild dogs at the gate;
Dost thou remember Sicily?

Still by the light and laughing sea
  Poor Polypheme bemoans his fate;
O Singer of Persephone!

And still in boyish rivalry
  Young Daphnis challenges his mate;
Dost thou remember Sicily?

Slim Lacon keeps a goat for thee,

For thee the jocund shepherds wait;

O Singer of Persephone!

Dost thou remember Sicily?

SONNETS

GREECE

The sea was sapphire coloured, and the sky
Burned like a heated opal through the air;
   We hoisted sail; the wind was blowing fair
For the blue lands that to the eastward lie.
From the steep prow I marked with quickening eye
   Zakynthos, every olive grove and creek,
   Ithaca's cliff, Lycaon's snowy peak,
And all the flower-strewn hills of Arcady.
The flapping of the sail against the mast,
   The ripple of the water on the side,
   The ripple of girls' laughter at the stern,
The only sounds:—when 'gan the West to burn,
   And a red sun upon the seas to ride,
   I stood upon the soil of Greece at last!

KATAKOLO.

PORTIA

TO ELLEN TERRY

(Written at the Lyceum Theatre)

I marvel not Bassanio was so bold

    To peril all he had upon the lead,

    Or that proud Aragon bent low his head

Or that Morocco's fiery heart grew cold:

For in that gorgeous dress of beaten gold

    Which is more golden than the golden sun

    No woman Veronesé looked upon

Was half so fair as thou whom I behold.

Yet fairer when with wisdom as your shield

    The sober-suited lawyer's gown you donned,

And would not let the laws of Venice yield

    Antonio's heart to that accursèd Jew—

    O Portia! take my heart: it is thy due:

I think I will not quarrel with the Bond.

FABIEN DEI FRANCHI

TO MY FRIEND HENRY IRVING

The silent room, the heavy creeping shade,

    The dead that travel fast, the opening door,

    The murdered brother rising through the floor,

    The ghost's white fingers on thy shoulders laid,

And then the lonely duel in the glade,

    The broken swords, the stifled scream, the gore,

    Thy grand revengeful eyes when all is o'er,—

These things are well enough,—but thou wert made

    For more august creation! frenzied Lear

    Should at thy bidding wander on the heath

    With the shrill fool to mock him, Romeo

For thee should lure his love, and desperate fear

Pluck Richard's recreant dagger from its sheath—

    Thou trumpet set for Shakespeare's lips to blow!

PHÈDRE

TO SARAH BERNHARDT

How vain and dull this common world must seem

    To such a One as thou, who should'st have talked

At Florence with Mirandola, or walked

Through the cool olives of the Academe:

Thou should'st have gathered reeds from a green stream

    For Goat-foot Pan's shrill piping, and have played

    With the white girls in that Phæacian glade

Where grave Odysseus wakened from his dream.

Ah! surely once some urn of Attic clay

    Held thy wan dust, and thou hast come again

Back to this common world so dull and vain,

For thou wert weary of the sunless day,

The heavy fields of scentless asphodel,

The loveless lips with which men kiss in Hell.

SONNET

ON HEARING THE DIES IRÆ SUNG IN THE SISTINE CHAPEL

Nay, Lord, not thus! white lilies in the spring,

Sad olive-groves, or silver-breasted dove,

Teach me more clearly of Thy life and love

Than terrors of red flame and thundering.

The hillside vines dear memories of Thee bring:

A bird at evening flying to its nest

Tells me of One who had no place of rest:

I think it is of Thee the sparrows sing.

Come rather on some autumn afternoon,

When red and brown are burnished on the leaves,

And the fields echo to the gleaner's song,

Come when the splendid fulness of the moon

Looks down upon the rows of golden sheaves,

And reap Thy harvest: we have waited long.

AVE MARIA GRATIA PLENA

Was this His coming! I had hoped to see

   A scene of wondrous glory, as was told

   Of some great God who in a rain of gold

Broke open bars and fell on Danae:

Or a dread vision as when Semele

   Sickening for love and unappeased desire

   Prayed to see God's clear body, and the fire

Caught her brown limbs and slew her utterly:

With such glad dreams I sought this holy place,

   And now with wondering eyes and heart I stand

   Before this supreme mystery of Love:

Some kneeling girl with passionless pale face,

   An angel with a lily in his hand,

   And over both the white wings of a Dove.

FLORENCE.

LIBERTATIS SACRA FAMES

Albeit nurtured in democracy,

   And liking best that state republican

   Where every man is Kinglike and no man

Is crowned above his fellows, yet I see,

Spite of this modern fret for Liberty,

   Better the rule of One, whom all obey,

   Than to let clamorous demagogues betray

Our freedom with the kiss of anarchy.

Wherefore I love them not whose hands profane

   Plant the red flag upon the piled-up street

   For no right cause, beneath whose ignorant reign

Arts, Culture, Reverence, Honour, all things fade,

   Save Treason and the dagger of her trade,

   Or Murder with his silent bloody feet.

ROSES AND RUE

(To L. L.)

Could we dig up this long-buried treasure,

   Were it worth the pleasure,

We never could learn love's song,

   We are parted too long.

Could the passionate past that is fled

   Call back its dead,

Could we live it all over again,

   Were it worth the pain!

I remember we used to meet
  By an ivied seat,
And you warbled each pretty word
  With the air of a bird;

And your voice had a quaver in it,
  Just like a linnet,
And shook, as the blackbird's throat
  With its last big note;

And your eyes, they were green and grey
  Like an April day,
But lit into amethyst
  When I stooped and kissed;

And your mouth, it would never smile
  For a long, long while,
Then it rippled all over with laughter
  Five minutes after.

You were always afraid of a shower,
  Just like a flower:

I remember you started and ran

    When the rain began.

I remember I never could catch you,

    For no one could match you,

You had wonderful, luminous, fleet,

    Little wings to your feet.

I remember your hair—did I tie it?

    For it always ran riot—

Like a tangled sunbeam of gold:

    These things are old.

I remember so well the room,

    And the lilac bloom

That beat at the dripping pane

    In the warm June rain;

And the colour of your gown,

    It was amber-brown,

And two yellow satin bows

    From your shoulders rose.

And the handkerchief of French lace

Which you held to your face—

Had a small tear left a stain?

　Or was it the rain?

On your hand as it waved adieu

　There were veins of blue;

In your voice as it said good-bye

　Was a petulant cry,

'You have only wasted your life.'

　(Ah, that was the knife!)

When I rushed through the garden gate

　It was all too late.

Could we live it over again,

　Were it worth the pain,

Could the passionate past that is fled

　Call back its dead!

Well, if my heart must break,

　Dear love, for your sake,

It will break in music, I know,

　Poets' hearts break so.

But strange that I was not told

That the brain can hold

In a tiny ivory cell

God's heaven and hell.

FROM 'THE GARDEN OF EROS'

[*In this poem the author laments the growth of materialism in the nineteenth century. He hails Keats and Shelley and some of the poets and artists who were his contemporaries, although his seniors, as the torch-bearers of the intellectual life. Among these are Swinburne, William Morris, Rossetti, and Brune-Jones.*]

Nay, when Keats died the Muses still had left

One silver voice to sing his threnody, [128]

But ah! too soon of it we were bereft

When on that riven night and stormy sea

Panthea claimed her singer as her own,

And slew the mouth that praised her; since which time we walk alone,

Save for that fiery heart, that morning star [129]

Of re-arisen England, whose clear eye

Saw from our tottering throne and waste of war

The grand Greek limbs of young Democracy

Rise mightily like Hesperus and bring

The great Republic! him at least thy love hath taught to sing,

And he hath been with thee at Thessaly,

    And seen white Atalanta fleet of foot

In passionless and fierce virginity

    Hunting the tuskèd boar, his honied lute

Hath pierced the cavern of the hollow hill,

And Venus laughs to know one knee will bow before her still.

And he hath kissed the lips of Proserpine,

    And sung the Galilæan's requiem,

That wounded forehead dashed with blood and wine

    He hath discrowned, the Ancient Gods in him

Have found their last, most ardent worshipper,

And the new Sign grows grey and dim before its conqueror.

Spirit of Beauty! tarry with us still,

    It is not quenched the torch of poesy,

The star that shook above the Eastern hill

    Holds unassailed its argent armoury

From all the gathering gloom and fretful fight—

O tarry with us still! for through the long and common night,

Morris, our sweet and simple Chaucer's child,

Dear heritor of Spenser's tuneful reed,

With soft and sylvan pipe has oft beguiled

The weary soul of man in troublous need,

And from the far and flowerless fields of ice

Has brought fair flowers to make an earthly paradise.

We know them all, Gudrun the strong men's bride,

Aslaug and Olafson we know them all,

How giant Grettir fought and Sigurd died,

And what enchantment held the king in thrall

When lonely Brynhild wrestled with the powers

That war against all passion, ah! how oft through summer hours,

Long listless summer hours when the noon

Being enamoured of a damask rose

Forgets to journey westward, till the moon

The pale usurper of its tribute grows

From a thin sickle to a silver shield

And chides its loitering car—how oft, in some cool grassy field

Far from the cricket-ground and noisy eight,

At Bagley, where the rustling bluebells come

Almost before the blackbird finds a mate

186

And overstay the swallow, and the hum

Of many murmuring bees flits through the leaves,

Have I lain poring on the dreamy tales his fancy weaves,

And through their unreal woes and mimic pain

   Wept for myself, and so was purified,

And in their simple mirth grew glad again;

   For as I sailed upon that pictured tide

The strength and splendour of the storm was mine

Without the storm's red ruin, for the singer is divine;

The little laugh of water falling down

   Is not so musical, the clammy gold

Close hoarded in the tiny waxen town

   Has less of sweetness in it, and the old

Half-withered reeds that waved in Arcady

Touched by his lips break forth again to fresher harmony.

Spirit of Beauty, tarry yet awhile!

   Although the cheating merchants of the mart

With iron roads profane our lovely isle,

   And break on whirling wheels the limbs of Art,

Ay! though the crowded factories beget

The blindworm Ignorance that slays the soul, O tarry yet!

For One at least there is,—He bears his name

From Dante and the seraph Gabriel,—[136]

Whose double laurels burn with deathless flame

To light thine altar; He [137] too loves thee well,

Who saw old Merlin lured in Vivien's snare,

And the white feet of angels coming down the golden stair,

Loves thee so well, that all the World for him

A gorgeous-coloured vestiture must wear,

And Sorrow take a purple diadem,

Or else be no more Sorrow, and Despair

Gild its own thorns, and Pain, like Adon, be

Even in anguish beautiful;—such is the empery

Which Painters hold, and such the heritage

This gentle solemn Spirit doth possess,

Being a better mirror of his age

In all his pity, love, and weariness,

Than those who can but copy common things,

And leave the Soul unpainted with its mighty questionings.

But they are few, and all romance has flown,

And men can prophesy about the sun,

And lecture on his arrows—how, alone,

Through a waste void the soulless atoms run,

How from each tree its weeping nymph has fled,

And that no more 'mid English reeds a Naiad shows her head.

THE HARLOT'S HOUSE

We caught the tread of dancing feet,

We loitered down the moonlit street,

And stopped beneath the harlot's house.

Inside, above the din and fray,

We heard the loud musicians play

The 'Treues Liebes Herz' of Strauss.

Like strange mechanical grotesques,

Making fantastic arabesques,

The shadows raced across the blind.

We watched the ghostly dancers spin

To sound of horn and violin,

Like black leaves wheeling in the wind.

Like wire-pulled automatons,

Slim silhouetted skeletons

Went sidling through the slow quadrille,

Then took each other by the hand,

And danced a stately saraband;

Their laughter echoed thin and shrill.

Sometimes a clockwork puppet pressed

A phantom lover to her breast,

Sometimes they seemed to try to sing.

Sometimes a horrible marionette

Came out, and smoked its cigarette

Upon the steps like a live thing.

Then, turning to my love, I said,

'The dead are dancing with the dead,

The dust is whirling with the dust.'

But she—she heard the violin,

And left my side, and entered in:

Love passed into the house of lust.

Then suddenly the tune went false,

The dancers wearied of the waltz,

The shadows ceased to wheel and whirl.

And down the long and silent street,

The dawn, with silver-sandalled feet,

Crept like a frightened girl.

FROM 'THE BURDEN OF ITYS'

This English Thames is holier far than Rome,

   Those harebells like a sudden flush of sea

Breaking across the woodland, with the foam

   Of meadow-sweet and white anemone

To fleck their blue waves,—God is likelier there

Than hidden in that crystal-hearted star the pale monks bear!

Those violet-gleaming butterflies that take

   Yon creamy lily for their pavilion

Are monsignores, and where the rushes shake

   A lazy pike lies basking in the sun,

His eyes half shut,—he is some mitred old

Bishop in partibus! look at those gaudy scales all green and gold.

The wind the restless prisoner of the trees

   Does well for Palæstrina, one would say

The mighty master's hands were on the keys

    Of the Maria organ, which they play

When early on some sapphire Easter morn

In a high litter red as blood or sin the Pope is borne

From his dark House out to the Balcony

    Above the bronze gates and the crowded square,

Whose very fountains seem for ecstasy

    To toss their silver lances in the air,

And stretching out weak hands to East and West

In vain sends peace to peaceless lands, to restless nations rest.

Is not yon lingering orange after-glow

    That stays to vex the moon more fair than all

Rome's lordliest pageants! strange, a year ago

    I knelt before some crimson Cardinal

Who bare the Host across the Esquiline,

And now—those common poppies in the wheat seem twice as fine.

The blue-green beanfields yonder, tremulous

    With the last shower, sweeter perfume bring

Through this cool evening than the odorous

    Flame-jewelled censers the young deacons swing,

When the grey priest unlocks the curtained shrine,

And makes God's body from the common fruit of corn and vine.

Poor Fra Giovanni bawling at the Mass

    Were out of tune now, for a small brown bird

Sings overhead, and through the long cool grass

    I see that throbbing throat which once I heard

On starlit hills of flower-starred Arcady,

Once where the white and crescent sand of Salamis meets sea.

Sweet is the swallow twittering on the eaves

    At daybreak, when the mower whets his scythe,

And stock-doves murmur, and the milkmaid leaves

    Her little lonely bed, and carols blithe

To see the heavy-lowing cattle wait

Stretching their huge and dripping mouths across the farmyard gate.

And sweet the hops upon the Kentish leas,

    And sweet the wind that lifts the new-mown hay,

And sweet the fretful swarms of grumbling bees

    That round and round the linden blossoms play;

And sweet the heifer breathing in the stall,

And the green bursting figs that hang upon the red-brick wall,

And sweet to hear the cuckoo mock the spring

　　While the last violet loiters by the well,

And sweet to hear the shepherd Daphnis sing

　　The song of Linus through a sunny dell

Of warm Arcadia where the corn is gold

And the slight lithe-limbed reapers dance about the wattled fold.

* * * * *

It was a dream, the glade is tenantless,

　　No soft Ionian laughter moves the air,

The Thames creeps on in sluggish leadenness,

　　And from the copse left desolate and bare

Fled is young Bacchus with his revelry,

Yet still from Nuneham wood there comes that thrilling melody

So sad, that one might think a human heart

　　Brake in each separate note, a quality

Which music sometimes has, being the Art

　　Which is most nigh to tears and memory;

Poor mourning Philomel, what dost thou fear?

Thy sister doth not haunt these fields, Pandion is not here,

Here is no cruel Lord with murderous blade,

No woven web of bloody heraldries,

But mossy dells for roving comrades made,

Warm valleys where the tired student lies

With half-shut book, and many a winding walk

Where rustic lovers stray at eve in happy simple talk.

The harmless rabbit gambols with its young

Across the trampled towing-path, where late

A troop of laughing boys in jostling throng

Cheered with their noisy cries the racing eight;

The gossamer, with ravelled silver threads,

Works at its little loom, and from the dusky red-eaved sheds

Of the lone Farm a flickering light shines out

Where the swinked shepherd drives his bleating flock

Back to their wattled sheep-cotes, a faint shout

Comes from some Oxford boat at Sandford lock,

And starts the moor-hen from the sedgy rill,

And the dim lengthening shadows flit like swallows up the hill.

The heron passes homeward to the mere,

The blue mist creeps among the shivering trees,

Gold world by world the silent stars appear,

And like a blossom blown before the breeze

A white moon drifts across the shimmering sky,

Mute arbitress of all thy sad, thy rapturous threnody.

She does not heed thee, wherefore should she heed,

   She knows Endymion is not far away;

'Tis I, 'tis I, whose soul is as the reed

   Which has no message of its own to play,

So pipes another's bidding, it is I,

Drifting with every wind on the wide sea of misery.

Ah! the brown bird has ceased: one exquisite trill

   About the sombre woodland seems to cling

Dying in music, else the air is still,

   So still that one might hear the bat's small wing

Wander and wheel above the pines, or tell

Each tiny dew-drop dripping from the bluebell's brimming cell.

And far away across the lengthening wold,

   Across the willowy flats and thickets brown,

Magdalen's tall tower tipped with tremulous gold

   Marks the long High Street of the little town,

And warns me to return; I must not wait,

   Hark! 't is the curfew booming from the bell at Christ Church gate.

FLOWER OF LOVE

Sweet, I blame you not, for mine the fault

was, had I not been made of common clay

I had climbed the higher heights unclimbed

yet, seen the fuller air, the larger day.

From the wildness of my wasted passion I had

struck a better, clearer song,

Lit some lighter light of freer freedom, battled

with some Hydra-headed wrong.

Had my lips been smitten into music by the

kisses that but made them bleed,

You had walked with Bice and the angels on

that verdant and enamelled mead.

I had trod the road which Dante treading saw

the suns of seven circles shine,

Ay! perchance had seen the heavens opening,

as they opened to the Florentine.

And the mighty nations would have crowned

me, who am crownless now and without name,

And some orient dawn had found me kneeling

on the threshold of the House of Fame.

I had sat within that marble circle where the

oldest bard is as the young,

And the pipe is ever dropping honey, and the

lyre's strings are ever strung.

Keats had lifted up his hymeneal curls from out

the poppy-seeded wine,

With ambrosial mouth had kissed my forehead,

clasped the hand of noble love in mine.

And at springtide, when the apple-blossoms

brush the burnished bosom of the dove,

Two young lovers lying in an orchard would

have read the story of our love;

Would have read the legend of my passion,

known the bitter secret of my heart,

Kissed as we have kissed, but never parted as

we two are fated now to part.

For the crimson flower of our life is eaten by

the cankerworm of truth,

And no hand can gather up the fallen withered

petals of the rose of youth.

Yet I am not sorry that I loved you—ah!

what else had I a boy to do,—

For the hungry teeth of time devour, and the

silent-footed years pursue.

Rudderless, we drift athwart a tempest, and

when once the storm of youth is past,

Without lyre, without lute or chorus, Death

the silent pilot comes at last.

And within the grave there is no pleasure,

for the blindworm battens on the root,

And Desire shudders into ashes, and the tree

of Passion bears no fruit.

Ah! what else had I to do but love you?

God's own mother was less dear to me,

And less dear the Cytheræan rising like an

argent lily from the sea.

I have made my choice, have lived my

poems, and, though youth is gone in wasted days,

I have found the lover's crown of myrtle better

than the poet's crown of bays.

FOOTNOTES

[128] Shelley.

[129] Swinburne.

[136] Rossetti.

[137] Burne-Jones.

About Author

Oscar Fingal O'Flahertie Wills Wilde (16 October 1854 – 30 November 1900) was an Irish poet and playwright. After writing in different forms throughout the 1880s, the early 1890s saw him become one of the most popular playwrights in London. He is best remembered for his epigrams and plays, his novel The Picture of Dorian Gray, and the circumstances of his criminal conviction for "gross indecency", imprisonment, and early death at age 46.

Wilde's parents were successful Anglo-Irish intellectuals in Dublin. A young Wilde learned to speak fluent French and German. At university, Wilde read Greats; he demonstrated himself to be an exceptional classicist, first at Trinity College Dublin, then at Oxford. He became associated with the emerging philosophy of aestheticism, led by two of his tutors, Walter Pater and John Ruskin. After university, Wilde moved to London into fashionable cultural and social circles.

As a spokesman for aestheticism, he tried his hand at various literary activities: he published a book of poems, lectured in the United States and Canada on the new "English Renaissance in Art" and interior decoration, and then returned to London where he worked prolifically as a journalist. Known for his biting wit, flamboyant dress and glittering conversational skill, Wilde became one of the best-known personalities of his day. At the turn of the 1890s, he refined his ideas about the supremacy of art in a series of dialogues and essays, and incorporated themes of decadence, duplicity, and beauty into what would be his only novel, The Picture of Dorian Gray (1890). The opportunity to construct aesthetic details precisely, and combine them with larger social themes, drew Wilde to write drama. He wrote Salome (1891) in French while in Paris but it was refused a licence for England due to an absolute prohibition on the portrayal of Biblical subjects on the English stage. Unperturbed, Wilde produced four society comedies in the early 1890s, which made him one of the most successful playwrights of late-Victorian London.

At the height of his fame and success, while The Importance of Being Earnest (1895) was still being performed in London, Wilde had the Marquess of Queensberry prosecuted for criminal libel. The Marquess was the father of Wilde's lover, Lord Alfred Douglas. The libel trial unearthed evidence that caused Wilde to drop his charges and led to his own arrest and trial for gross indecency with men. After two more trials he was convicted and sentenced to two years' hard labour, the maximum penalty, and was jailed from 1895 to 1897. During his last year in prison, he wrote De Profundis (published posthumously in 1905), a long letter which discusses his spiritual journey through his trials, forming a dark counterpoint to his earlier philosophy of pleasure. On his release, he left immediately for France, never to return to Ireland or Britain. There he wrote his last work, The Ballad of Reading Gaol (1898), a long poem commemorating the harsh rhythms of prison life.

Early life

Oscar Wilde was born at 21 Westland Row, Dublin (now home of the Oscar Wilde Centre, Trinity College), the second of three children born to Anglo-Irish Sir William Wilde and Jane Wilde, two years behind his brother William ("Willie"). Wilde's mother had distant Italian ancestry,and under the pseudonym "Speranza" (the Italian word for 'hope'), wrote poetry for the revolutionary Young Irelanders in 1848; she was a lifelong Irish nationalist. She read the Young Irelanders' poetry to Oscar and Willie, inculcating a love of these poets in her sons. Lady Wilde's interest in the neo-classical revival showed in the paintings and busts of ancient Greece and Rome in her home.

William Wilde was Ireland's leading oto-ophthalmologic (ear and eye) surgeon and was knighted in 1864 for his services as medical adviser and assistant commissioner to the censuses of Ireland. He also wrote books about Irish archaeology and peasant folklore. A renowned philanthropist, his dispensary for the care of the city's poor at the rear of Trinity College, Dublin, was the forerunner of the Dublin Eye and Ear Hospital, now located at Adelaide Road. On his father's side Wilde was descended from a Dutchman, Colonel de Wilde, who went to Ireland with King William of Orange's invading army in 1690, and numerous Anglo-Irish ancestors. On his mother's side, Wilde's ancestors included a bricklayer from County Durham, who emigrated to Ireland sometime in the 1770s.

Wilde was baptised as an infant in St. Mark's Church, Dublin, the local Church of Ireland (Anglican) church. When the church was closed, the records were moved to the nearby St. Ann's Church, Dawson Street. Davis Coakley mentions a second baptism by a Catholic priest, Father Prideaux Fox, who befriended Oscar's mother circa 1859. According to Fox's testimony in Donahoe's Magazine in 1905, Jane Wilde would visit his chapel in Glencree, County Wicklow, for Mass and would take her sons with her. She asked Father Fox in this period to baptise her sons.

Fox described it in this way:

"I am not sure if she ever became a Catholic herself but it was not long before she asked me to instruct two of her children, one of them being the future erratic genius, Oscar Wilde. After a few weeks I baptized these two children, Lady Wilde herself being present on the occasion.

In addition to his children with his wife, Sir William Wilde was the father of three children born out of wedlock before his marriage: Henry Wilson, born in 1838 to one woman, and Emily and Mary Wilde, born in 1847 and 1849, respectively, to a second woman. Sir William acknowledged paternity of his illegitimate or "natural" children and provided for their education, arranging for them to be reared by his relatives rather than with his legitimate children in his family household with his wife.

In 1855, the family moved to No. 1 Merrion Square, where Wilde's sister, Isola, was born in 1857. The Wildes' new home was larger. With both his parents' success and delight in social life, the house soon became the site of a "unique medical and cultural milieu". Guests at their salon included Sheridan Le Fanu, Charles Lever, George Petrie, Isaac Butt, William Rowan Hamilton and Samuel Ferguson.

Until he was nine, Oscar Wilde was educated at home, where a French nursemaid and a German governess taught him their languages. He attended Portora Royal School in Enniskillen, County Fermanagh, from 1864 to 1871. Until his early twenties, Wilde summered at the villa, Moytura House, which his father had built in Cong, County Mayo. There the young Wilde and his brother Willie played with George Moore.

Isola died at age nine of meningitis. Wilde's poem "Requiescat" is written to her memory.

"Tread lightly, she is near

Under the snow

Speak gently, she can hear

the daisies grow"

University education: 1870s

Trinity College, Dublin

Wilde left Portora with a royal scholarship to read classics at Trinity College, Dublin, from 1871 to 1874, sharing rooms with his older brother Willie Wilde. Trinity, one of the leading classical schools, placed him with scholars such as R. Y. Tyrell, Arthur Palmer, Edward Dowden and his tutor, Professor J. P. Mahaffy, who inspired his interest in Greek literature. As a student Wilde worked with Mahaffy on the latter's book Social Life in Greece. Wilde, despite later reservations, called Mahaffy "my first and best teacher" and "the scholar who showed me how to love Greek things".For his part, Mahaffy boasted of having created Wilde; later, he said Wilde was "the only blot on my tutorship".

The University Philosophical Society also provided an education, as members discussed intellectual and artistic subjects such as Dante Gabriel Rossetti and Algernon Charles Swinburne weekly. Wilde quickly became an established member – the members' suggestion book for 1874 contains two pages of banter (sportingly) mocking Wilde's emergent aestheticism. He presented a paper titled "Aesthetic Morality". At Trinity, Wilde established himself as an outstanding student: he came first in his class in his first year, won a scholarship by competitive examination in his second and, in his finals, won the Berkeley Gold Medal in Greek, the University's highest academic award. He was encouraged to compete for a demyship to Magdalen College, Oxford – which he won easily, having already studied Greek for over nine years.

Magdalen College, Oxford

At Magdalen, he read Greats from 1874 to 1878, and from there he applied to join the Oxford Union, but failed to be elected.

Attracted by its dress, secrecy, and ritual, Wilde petitioned the Apollo Masonic Lodge at Oxford, and was soon raised to the "Sublime Degree of Master Mason".During a resurgent interest in Freemasonry in his third year, he commented he "would be awfully sorry to give it up if I secede from the Protestant Heresy". Wilde's active involvement in Freemasonry lasted only for the time he spent at Oxford; he allowed his membership of the Apollo University Lodge to lapse after failing to pay subscriptions.

Catholicism deeply appealed to him, especially its rich liturgy, and he discussed converting to it with clergy several times. In 1877, Wilde was left speechless after an audience with Pope Pius IX in Rome.He eagerly read the books of Cardinal Newman, a noted Anglican priest who had converted to Catholicism and risen in the church hierarchy. He became more serious in 1878, when he met the Reverend Sebastian Bowden, a priest in the Brompton Oratory who had received some high-profile converts. Neither his father, who threatened to cut off his funds, nor Mahaffy thought much of the plan; but mostly Wilde, the supreme individualist, balked at the last minute from pledging himself to any formal creed. On the appointed day of his baptism, Wilde sent Father Bowden a bunch of altar lilies instead. Wilde did retain a lifelong interest in Catholic theology and liturgy.

While at Magdalen College, Wilde became particularly well known for his role in the aesthetic and decadent movements. He wore his hair long, openly scorned "manly" sports though he occasionally boxed, and he decorated his rooms with peacock feathers, lilies, sunflowers, blue china and other objets d'art. He once remarked to friends, whom he entertained lavishly, "I find it harder and harder every day to live up to my blue china." The line quickly became famous, accepted as a slogan by aesthetes but used against them by critics who sensed in it a terrible vacuousness. Some elements disdained the aesthetes, but their languishing attitudes and showy costumes became a recognised pose. Wilde was once physically attacked by a group of four fellow students, and dealt with them single-handedly, surprising critics. By his third year Wilde had truly begun to develop himself and his myth, and considered his learning to be more expansive than what was within the prescribed texts. This attitude resulted in his being rusticated for one term, after he had returned late to a college term from a trip to Greece with Mahaffy.

Wilde did not meet Walter Pater until his third year, but had been enthralled by his Studies in the History of the Renaissance, published during Wilde's final year in Trinity. Pater argued that man's sensibility to beauty should be refined above all else, and that each moment should be felt to its fullest extent. Years later, in De Profundis, Wilde described Pater's Studies... as "that book that has had such a strange influence over my life".He learned tracts of the book by heart, and carried it with him on travels in later years. Pater gave Wilde his sense of almost flippant devotion to art, though he gained a purpose for it through the lectures and writings of critic John Ruskin. Ruskin despaired at the self-validating aestheticism of Pater, arguing that the importance of art lies in its potential for the betterment of society. Ruskin admired beauty, but believed it must be allied with, and applied to, moral good. When Wilde eagerly attended Ruskin's lecture series The Aesthetic and Mathematic Schools of Art in Florence, he learned about aesthetics as the non-mathematical elements of painting. Despite being given to neither early rising nor manual labour, Wilde volunteered for Ruskin's project to convert a swampy country lane into a smart road neatly edged with flowers.

Wilde won the 1878 Newdigate Prize for his poem "Ravenna", which reflected on his visit there the year before, and he duly read it at Encaenia. In November 1878, he graduated with a double first in his B.A. of Classical Moderations and Literae Humaniores (Greats). Wilde wrote to a friend, "The dons are 'astonied' beyond words – the Bad Boy doing so well in the end!"

Apprenticeship of an aesthete: 1880s

Debut in society

After graduation from Oxford, Wilde returned to Dublin, where he met again Florence Balcombe, a childhood sweetheart. She became engaged to Bram Stoker and they married in 1878. Wilde was disappointed but stoic:

he wrote to her, remembering "the two sweet years – the sweetest years of all my youth" during which they had been close. He also stated his intention to "return to England, probably for good." This he did in 1878, only briefly visiting Ireland twice after that.

Unsure of his next step, Wilde wrote to various acquaintances enquiring about Classics positions at Oxford or Cambridge. The Rise of Historical Criticism was his submission for the Chancellor's Essay prize of 1879, which, though no longer a student, he was still eligible to enter. Its subject, "Historical Criticism among the Ancients" seemed ready-made for Wilde – with both his skill in composition and ancient learning – but he struggled to find his voice with the long, flat, scholarly style. Unusually, no prize was awarded that year.

With the last of his inheritance from the sale of his father's houses, he set himself up as a bachelor in London. The 1881 British Census listed Wilde as a boarder at 1 (now 44) Tite Street, Chelsea, where Frank Miles, a society painter, was the head of the household. Wilde spent the next six years in London and Paris, and in the United States, where he travelled to deliver lectures.

He had been publishing lyrics and poems in magazines since entering Trinity College, especially in Kottabos and the Dublin University Magazine. In mid-1881, at 27 years old, he published Poems, which collected, revised and expanded his poems.

The book was generally well received, and sold out its first print run of 750 copies. Punch was less enthusiastic, saying "The poet is Wilde, but his poetry's tame". By a tight vote, the Oxford Union condemned the book for alleged plagiarism. The librarian, who had requested the book for the library, returned the presentation copy to Wilde with a note of apology.Biographer Richard Ellmann argues that Wilde's poem "Hélas!" was a sincere, though flamboyant, attempt to explain the dichotomies the poet saw in himself; one line reads: "To drift with every passion till my soul

Is a stringed lute on which all winds can play".

The book had further printings in 1882. It was bound in a rich, enamel parchment cover (embossed with gilt blossom) and printed on hand-made Dutch paper; over the next few years, Wilde presented many copies to the dignitaries and writers who received him during his lecture tours.

America: 1882

Aestheticism was sufficiently in vogue to be caricatured by Gilbert and Sullivan in Patience (1881). Richard D'Oyly Carte, an English impresario, invited Wilde to make a lecture tour of North America, simultaneously priming the pump for the US tour of Patience and selling this most charming aesthete to the American public. Wilde journeyed on the SS Arizona, arriving 2 January 1882, and disembarking the following day. Originally planned to last four months, it continued for almost a year due to the commercial success. Wilde sought to transpose the beauty he saw in art into daily life. This was a practical as well as philosophical project: in Oxford he had surrounded himself with blue china and lilies, and now one of his lectures was on interior design.

When asked to explain reports that he had paraded down Piccadilly in London carrying a lily, long hair flowing, Wilde replied, "It's not whether I did it or not that's important, but whether people believed I did it". Wilde believed that the artist should hold forth higher ideals, and that pleasure and beauty would replace utilitarian ethics.

Wilde and aestheticism were both mercilessly caricatured and criticised in the press; the Springfield Republican, for instance, commented on Wilde's behaviour during his visit to Boston to lecture on aestheticism, suggesting that Wilde's conduct was more a bid for notoriety rather than devotion to beauty and the aesthetic. T. W. Higginson, a cleric and abolitionist, wrote in "Unmanly Manhood" of his general concern that Wilde, "whose only distinction is that he has written a thin volume of very mediocre verse", would improperly influence the behaviour of men and women.

According to biographer Michèle Mendelssohn, Wilde was the subject of anti-Irish caricature and was portrayed as a monkey, a blackface performer and a Christy's Minstrel throughout his career. "Harper's Weekly put a sunflower-worshipping monkey dressed as Wilde on the front of the January 1882 issue. The magazine didn't let its reputation for quality impede its expression of what are now considered odious ethnic and racial ideologies. The drawing stimulated other American maligners and, in England, had a full-page reprint in the Lady's Pictorial. ... When the National Republican discussed Wilde, it was to explain 'a few items as to the animal's pedigree.' And on 22 January 1882 the Washington Post illustrated the Wild Man of Borneo alongside Oscar Wilde of England and asked 'How far is it from this to this?' "Though his press reception was hostile, Wilde was well received in diverse settings across America; he drank whiskey with miners in Leadville, Colorado, and was fêted at the most fashionable salons in many cities he visited.

London life and marriage

His earnings, plus expected income from The Duchess of Padua, allowed him to move to Paris between February and mid-May 1883. While there he met Robert Sherard, whom he entertained constantly. "We are dining on the Duchess tonight", Wilde would declare before taking him to an expensive restaurant. In August he briefly returned to New York for the production of Vera, his first play, after it was turned down in London. He reportedly entertained the other passengers with "Ave Imperatrix!, A Poem on England", about the rise and fall of empires. E. C. Stedman, in Victorian Poets, describes this "lyric to England" as "manly verse – a poetic and eloquent invocation". The play was initially well received by the audience, but when the critics wrote lukewarm reviews, attendance fell sharply and the play closed a week after it had opened.

Wilde had to return to England, where he continued to lecture on topics including Personal Impressions of America, The Value of Art in Modern Life, and Dress.

In London, he had been introduced in 1881 to Constance Lloyd, daughter of Horace Lloyd, a wealthy Queen's Counsel, and his wife. She happened to be visiting Dublin in 1884, when Wilde was lecturing at the Gaiety Theatre. He proposed to her, and they married on 29 May 1884 at the Anglican St James's Church, Paddington, in London. Although Constance had an annual allowance of £250, which was generous for a young woman (equivalent to about £25,600 in current value), the Wildes had relatively luxurious tastes. They had preached to others for so long on the subject of design that people expected their home to set new standards. No. 16, Tite Street was duly renovated in seven months at considerable expense. The couple had two sons together, Cyril (1885) and Vyvyan (1886). Wilde became the sole literary signatory of George Bernard Shaw's petition for a pardon of the anarchists arrested (and later executed) after the Haymarket massacre in Chicago in 1886.

Robert Ross had read Wilde's poems before they met at Oxford in 1886. He seemed unrestrained by the Victorian prohibition against homosexuality, and became estranged from his family. By Richard Ellmann's account, he was a precocious seventeen-year-old who "so young and yet so knowing, was determined to seduce Wilde". According to Daniel Mendelsohn, Wilde, who had long alluded to Greek love, was "initiated into homosexual sex" by Ross, while his "marriage had begun to unravel after his wife's second pregnancy, which left him physically repelled".

Prose writing: 1886–91

Journalism and editorship: 1886–89

Criticism over artistic matters in The Pall Mall Gazette provoked a letter in self-defence, and soon Wilde was a contributor to that and other journals during 1885–87. He enjoyed reviewing and journalism; the form suited his style. He could organise and share his views on art, literature and life, yet in a format less tedious than lecturing. Buoyed up, his reviews were largely chatty and positive. Wilde, like his parents before him, also supported the cause of Irish nationalism. When Charles Stewart Parnell was falsely accused of inciting murder, Wilde wrote a series of astute columns defending him in the Daily Chronicle.

His flair, having previously been put mainly into socialising, suited journalism and rapidly attracted notice. With his youth nearly over, and a family to support, in mid-1887 Wilde became the editor of The Lady's World magazine, his name prominently appearing on the cover. He promptly renamed it as The Woman's World and raised its tone, adding serious articles on parenting, culture, and politics, while keeping discussions of fashion and arts. Two pieces of fiction were usually included, one to be read to children, the other for the ladies themselves. Wilde worked hard to solicit good contributions from his wide artistic acquaintance, including those of Lady Wilde and his wife Constance, while his own "Literary and Other Notes" were themselves popular and amusing.

The initial vigour and excitement which he brought to the job began to fade as administration, commuting and office life became tedious. At the same time as Wilde's interest flagged, the publishers became concerned anew about circulation: sales, at the relatively high price of one shilling, remained low. Increasingly sending instructions to the magazine by letter, Wilde began a new period of creative work and his own column appeared less regularly.In October 1889, Wilde had finally found his voice in prose and, at the end of the second volume, Wilde left The Woman's World. The magazine outlasted him by one issue.

If Wilde's period at the helm of the magazine was a mixed success from an organizational point of view, it played a pivotal role in his development as a writer and facilitated his ascent to fame. Whilst Wilde the journalist supplied articles under the guidance of his editors, Wilde the editor was forced to learn to manipulate the literary marketplace on his own terms.

During the late 1880s, Wilde was a close friend of the artist James NcNeill Whistler and they dined together on many occasions. At one of these dinners, Whistler said a bon mot that Wilde found particularly witty, Wilde exclaimed that he wished that he had said it, and Whistler retorted "You will, Oscar, you will".Herbert Vivian—a mutual friend of Wilde and Whistler— attended the dinner and recorded it in his article The Reminiscences of a Short Life which appeared in The Sun in 1889. The article alleged that Wilde had a habit of passing off other people's witticisms as his own—especially Whistler's. Wilde considered Vivian's article to be a scurrilous betrayal, and it directly caused the broken friendship between Wilde and Whistler. The Reminiscences also caused great acrimony between Wilde and Vivian, Wilde accusing Vivian of "the inaccuracy of an eavesdropper with the method of a blackmailer" and banishing Vivian from his circle.

Shorter fiction

Wilde published The Happy Prince and Other Tales in 1888, and had been regularly writing fairy stories for magazines. In 1891 he published two more collections, Lord Arthur Savile's Crime and Other Stories, and in September A House of Pomegranates was dedicated "To Constance Mary Wilde". "The Portrait of Mr. W. H.", which Wilde had begun in 1887, was first published in Blackwood's Edinburgh Magazine in July 1889.It is a short story, which reports a conversation, in which the theory that Shakespeare's sonnets were written out of the poet's love of the boy actor "Willie Hughes", is advanced, retracted, and then propounded again. The only evidence for this is two supposed puns within the sonnets themselves.

The anonymous narrator is at first sceptical, then believing, finally flirtatious with the reader: he concludes that "there is really a great deal to be said of the Willie Hughes theory of Shakespeare's sonnets." By the end fact and fiction have melded together.Arthur Ransome wrote that Wilde "read something of himself into Shakespeare's sonnets" and became fascinated with the "Willie Hughes theory" despite the lack of biographical evidence for the historical William Hughes' existence. Instead of writing a short but serious essay on the question, Wilde tossed the theory amongst the three characters of the story, allowing it to unfold as background to the plot. The story thus is an early masterpiece of Wilde's combining many elements that interested him: conversation, literature and the idea that to shed oneself of an idea one must first convince another of its truth.Ransome concludes that Wilde succeeds precisely because the literary criticism is unveiled with such a deft touch.

Though containing nothing but "special pleading", it would not, he says "be possible to build an airier castle in Spain than this of the imaginary William Hughes" we continue listening nonetheless to be charmed by the telling. "You must believe in Willie Hughes," Wilde told an acquaintance, "I almost do, myself."

Essays and dialogues

Wilde, having tired of journalism, had been busy setting out his aesthetic ideas more fully in a series of longer prose pieces which were published in the major literary-intellectual journals of the day. In January 1889, The Decay of Lying: A Dialogue appeared in The Nineteenth Century, and Pen, Pencil and Poison, a satirical biography of Thomas Griffiths Wainewright, in The Fortnightly Review, edited by Wilde's friend Frank Harris. Two of Wilde's four writings on aesthetics are dialogues: though Wilde had evolved professionally from lecturer to writer, he retained an oral tradition of sorts. Having always excelled as a wit and raconteur, he often composed by assembling phrases, bons mots and witticisms into a longer, cohesive work.

Wilde was concerned about the effect of moralising on art; he believed in art's redemptive, developmental powers: "Art is individualism, and individualism is a disturbing and disintegrating force. There lies its immense value. For what it seeks is to disturb monotony of type, slavery of custom, tyranny of habit, and the reduction of man to the level of a machine." In his only political text, The Soul of Man Under Socialism, he argued political conditions should establish this primacy – private property should be abolished, and cooperation should be substituted for competition. At the same time, he stressed that the government most amenable to artists was no government at all. Wilde envisioned a society where mechanisation has freed human effort from the burden of necessity, effort which can instead be expended on artistic creation. George Orwell summarised, "In effect, the world will be populated by artists, each striving after perfection in the way that seems best to him."

This point of view did not align him with the Fabians, intellectual socialists who advocated using state apparatus to change social conditions, nor did it endear him to the monied classes whom he had previously entertained. Hesketh Pearson, introducing a collection of Wilde's essays in 1950, remarked how The Soul of Man Under Socialism had been an inspirational text for revolutionaries in Tsarist Russia but laments that in the Stalinist era "it is doubtful whether there are any uninspected places in which it could now be hidden".

Wilde considered including this pamphlet and The Portrait of Mr. W.H., his essay-story on Shakespeare's sonnets, in a new anthology in 1891, but eventually decided to limit it to purely aesthetic subjects. Intentions packaged revisions of four essays: The Decay of Lying, Pen, Pencil and Poison, The Truth of Masks (first published 1885), and The Critic as Artist in two parts. For Pearson the biographer, the essays and dialogues exhibit every aspect of Wilde's genius and character: wit, romancer, talker, lecturer, humanist and scholar and concludes that "no other productions of his have as varied an appeal". 1891 turned out to be Wilde's annus mirabilis; apart from his three collections he also produced his only novel.

The Picture of Dorian Gray

The first version of The Picture of Dorian Gray was published as the lead story in the July 1890 edition of Lippincott's Monthly Magazine, along with five others. The story begins with a man painting a picture of Gray. When Gray, who has a "face like ivory and rose leaves", sees his finished portrait, he breaks down. Distraught that his beauty will fade while the portrait stays beautiful, he inadvertently makes a Faustian bargain in which only the painted image grows old while he stays beautiful and young. For Wilde, the purpose of art would be to guide life as if beauty alone were its object. As Gray's portrait allows him to escape the corporeal ravages of his hedonism, Wilde sought to juxtapose the beauty he saw in art with daily life.

Reviewers immediately criticised the novel's decadence and homosexual allusions; The Daily Chronicle for example, called it "unclean", "poisonous", and "heavy with the mephitic odours of moral and spiritual putrefaction". Which he clarified his stance on ethics and aesthetics in art – "If a work of art is rich and vital and complete, those who have artistic instincts will see its beauty and those to whom ethics appeal more strongly will see its moral lesson." He nevertheless revised it extensively for book publication in 1891: six new chapters were added, some overtly decadent passages and homo-eroticism excised, and a preface was included consisting of twenty two epigrams, such as "Books are well written, or badly written. That is all."

Contemporary reviewers and modern critics have postulated numerous possible sources of the story, a search Jershua McCormack argues is futile because Wilde "has tapped a root of Western folklore so deep and ubiquitous that the story has escaped its origins and returned to the oral tradition." Wilde claimed the plot was "an idea that is as old as the history of literature but to which I have given a new form".Modern critic Robin McKie considered the novel to be technically mediocre, saying that the conceit of the plot had guaranteed its fame, but the device is never pushed to its full.On the other hand, Robert McCrum of The Guardian deemed it the 27th best novel ever written in English, calling it "an arresting, and slightly camp, exercise in late-Victorian gothic."

Theatrical career: 1892–95

Salomé

The 1891 census records the Wildes' residence at 16 Tite Street, where he lived with his wife Constance and two sons. Wilde though, not content with being better known than ever in London, returned to Paris in October 1891, this time as a respected writer. He was received at the salons littéraires, including the famous mardis of Stéphane Mallarmé, a renowned symbolist poet of the time. Wilde's two plays during the 1880s, Vera; or, The Nihilists and The Duchess of Padua, had not met with much success. He had continued his interest in the theatre and now, after finding his voice in prose, his thoughts turned again to the dramatic form as the biblical iconography of Salome filled his mind. One evening, after discussing depictions of Salome throughout history, he returned to his hotel and noticed a blank copybook lying on the desk, and it occurred to him to write in it what he had been saying. The result was a new play, Salomé, written rapidly and in French.

A tragedy, it tells the story of Salome, the stepdaughter of the tetrarch Herod Antipas, who, to her stepfather's dismay but mother's delight, requests the head of Jokanaan (John the Baptist) on a silver platter as a reward for dancing the Dance of the Seven Veils. When Wilde returned to London just before Christmas the Paris Echo referred to him as "le great event" of the season. Rehearsals of the play, starring Sarah Bernhardt, began but the play was refused a licence by the Lord Chamberlain, since it depicted biblical characters. Salome was published jointly in Paris and London in 1893, but was not performed until 1896 in Paris, during Wilde's later incarceration.

Comedies of society

Wilde, who had first set out to irritate Victorian society with his dress and talking points, then outrage it with Dorian Gray, his novel of vice hidden beneath art, finally found a way to critique society on its own terms. Lady Windermere's Fan was first performed on 20 February 1892 at St James's Theatre, packed with the cream of society. On the surface a witty comedy, there is subtle subversion underneath: "it concludes with collusive concealment rather than collective disclosure". The audience, like Lady Windermere, are forced to soften harsh social codes in favour of a more nuanced view. The play was enormously popular, touring the country for months, but largely trashed by conservative critics. It was followed by A Woman of No Importance in 1893, another Victorian comedy, revolving around the spectre of illegitimate births, mistaken identities and late revelations. Wilde was commissioned to write two more plays and An Ideal Husband, written in 1894, followed in January 1895.

Peter Raby said these essentially English plays were well-pitched, "Wilde, with one eye on the dramatic genius of Ibsen, and the other on the commercial competition in London's West End, targeted his audience with adroit precision".

Queensberry family

In mid-1891 Lionel Johnson introduced Wilde to Lord Alfred Douglas, Johnson's cousin and an undergraduate at Oxford at the time. Known to his family and friends as "Bosie", he was a handsome and spoilt young man. An intimate friendship sprang up between Wilde and Douglas and by 1893 Wilde was infatuated with Douglas and they consorted together regularly in a tempestuous affair. If Wilde was relatively indiscreet, even flamboyant, in the way he acted, Douglas was reckless in public. Wilde, who was earning up to £100 a week from his plays (his salary at The Woman's World had been £6), indulged Douglas's every whim: material, artistic or sexual.

Douglas soon initiated Wilde into the Victorian underground of gay prostitution and Wilde was introduced to a series of young working-class male prostitutes from 1892 onwards by Alfred Taylor. These infrequent rendezvous usually took the same form: Wilde would meet the boy, offer him gifts, dine him privately and then take him to a hotel room. Unlike Wilde's idealised relations with Ross, John Gray, and Douglas, all of whom remained part of his aesthetic circle, these consorts were uneducated and knew nothing of literature. Soon his public and private lives had become sharply divided; in De Profundis he wrote to Douglas that "It was like feasting with panthers; the danger was half the excitement... I did not know that when they were to strike at me it was to be at another's piping and at another's pay."

Douglas and some Oxford friends founded a journal, The Chameleon, to which Wilde "sent a page of paradoxes originally destined for the Saturday Review". "Phrases and Philosophies for the Use of the Young" was to come under attack six months later at Wilde's trial, where he was forced to defend the magazine to which he had sent his work.In any case, it became unique: The Chameleon was not published again.

Lord Alfred's father, the Marquess of Queensberry, was known for his outspoken atheism, brutish manner and creation of the modern rules of boxing. Queensberry, who feuded regularly with his son, confronted Wilde and Lord Alfred about the nature of their relationship several times, but Wilde was able to mollify him. In June 1894, he called on Wilde at 16 Tite Street, without an appointment, and clarified his stance: "I do not say that you are it, but you look it, and pose at it, which is just as bad. And if I catch you and my son again in any public restaurant I will thrash you" to which Wilde responded: "I don't know what the Queensberry rules are, but the Oscar Wilde rule is to shoot on sight".His account in De Profundis was less triumphant: "It was when, in my library at Tite Street, waving his small hands in the air in epileptic fury, your father... stood uttering every foul word his foul mind could think of, and screaming the loathsome threats he afterwards with such cunning carried out". Queensberry only described the scene once, saying Wilde had "shown him the white feather", meaning he had acted in a cowardly way. Though trying to remain calm, Wilde saw that he was becoming ensnared in a brutal family quarrel. He did not wish to bear Queensberry's insults, but he knew to confront him could lead to disaster were his liaisons disclosed publicly.

The Importance of Being Earnest

Wilde's final play again returns to the theme of switched identities: the play's two protagonists engage in "bunburying" (the maintenance of alternative personas in the town and country) which allows them to escape Victorian social mores.Earnest is even lighter in tone than Wilde's earlier comedies. While their characters often rise to serious themes in moments of crisis, Earnest lacks the by-now stock Wildean characters: there is no "woman with a past", the principals are neither villainous nor cunning, simply idle cultivés, and the idealistic young women are not that innocent. Mostly set in drawing rooms and almost completely lacking in action or violence, Earnest lacks the self-conscious decadence found in The Picture of Dorian Gray and Salome.

The play, now considered Wilde's masterpiece, was rapidly written in Wilde's artistic maturity in late 1894. It was first performed on 14 February 1895, at St James's Theatre in London, Wilde's second collaboration with George Alexander, the actor-manager. Both author and producer assiduously revised, prepared and rehearsed every line, scene and setting in the months before the premiere, creating a carefully constructed representation of late-Victorian society, yet simultaneously mocking it. During rehearsal Alexander requested that Wilde shorten the play from four acts to three, which the author did. Premieres at St James's seemed like "brilliant parties", and the opening of The Importance of Being Earnest was no exception. Allan Aynesworth (who played Algernon) recalled to Hesketh Pearson, "In my fifty-three years of acting, I never remember a greater triumph than [that] first night."Earnest's immediate reception as Wilde's best work to date finally crystallised his fame into a solid artistic reputation. The Importance of Being Earnest remains his most popular play.

Wilde's professional success was mirrored by an escalation in his feud with Queensberry. Queensberry had planned to insult Wilde publicly by throwing a bouquet of rotting vegetables onto the stage; Wilde was tipped off and had Queensberry barred from entering the theatre.Fifteen weeks later Wilde was in prison.

Trials

220

Wilde v. Queensberry

On 18 February 1895, the Marquess left his calling card at Wilde's club, the Albemarle, inscribed: "For Oscar Wilde, posing somdomite" Wilde, encouraged by Douglas and against the advice of his friends, initiated a private prosecution against Queensberry for libel, since the note amounted to a public accusation that Wilde had committed the crime of sodomy.

Queensberry was arrested for criminal libel; a charge carrying a possible sentence of up to two years in prison. Under the 1843 Libel Act, Queensberry could avoid conviction for libel only by demonstrating that his accusation was in fact true, and furthermore that there was some "public benefit" to having made the accusation openly. Queensberry's lawyers thus hired private detectives to find evidence of Wilde's homosexual liaisons.

Wilde's friends had advised him against the prosecution at a Saturday Review meeting at the Café Royal on 24 March 1895; Frank Harris warned him that "they are going to prove sodomy against you" and advised him to flee to France. Wilde and Douglas walked out in a huff, Wilde saying "it is at such moments as these that one sees who are one's true friends". The scene was witnessed by George Bernard Shaw who recalled it to Arthur Ransome a day or so before Ransome's trial for libelling Douglas in 1913. To Ransome it confirmed what he had said in his 1912 book on Wilde; that Douglas's rivalry for Wilde with Robbie Ross and his arguments with his father had resulted in Wilde's public disaster; as Wilde wrote in De Profundis. Douglas lost his case. Shaw included an account of the argument between Harris, Douglas and Wilde in the preface to his play The Dark Lady of the Sonnets.

The libel trial became a cause célèbre as salacious details of Wilde's private life with Taylor and Douglas began to appear in the press. A team of private detectives had directed Queensberry's lawyers, led by Edward Carson QC, to the world of the Victorian underground. Wilde's association with blackmailers and male prostitutes, cross-dressers and homosexual brothels was recorded, and various persons involved were interviewed, some being coerced to appear as witnesses since they too were accomplices to the crimes of which Wilde was accused.

The trial opened on 3 April 1895 before Justice Richard Henn Collins amid scenes of near hysteria both in the press and the public galleries. The extent of the evidence massed against Wilde forced him to declare meekly, "I am the prosecutor in this case" Wilde's lawyer, Sir Edward George Clarke, opened the case by pre-emptively asking Wilde about two suggestive letters Wilde had written to Douglas, which the defence had in its possession. He characterised the first as a "prose sonnet" and admitted that the "poetical language" might seem strange to the court but claimed its intent was innocent. Wilde stated that the letters had been obtained by blackmailers who had attempted to extort money from him, but he had refused, suggesting they should take the £60 (equal to £6,800 today) offered, "unusual for a prose piece of that length". He claimed to regard the letters as works of art rather than something of which to be ashamed.

Carson, a fellow Dubliner who had attended Trinity College, Dublin at the same time as Wilde, cross-examined Wilde on how he perceived the moral content of his works. Wilde replied with characteristic wit and flippancy, claiming that works of art are not capable of being moral or immoral but only well or poorly made, and that only "brutes and illiterates", whose views on art "are incalculably stupid", would make such judgements about art. Carson, a leading barrister, diverged from the normal practice of asking closed questions. Carson pressed Wilde on each topic from every angle, squeezing out nuances of meaning from Wilde's answers, removing them from their aesthetic context and portraying Wilde as evasive and decadent. While Wilde won the most laughs from the court, Carson scored the most legal points. To undermine Wilde's credibility, and to justify Queensberry's description of Wilde as a "posing somdomite", Carson drew from the witness an admission of his capacity for "posing", by demonstrating that he had lied about his age on oath. Playing on this, he returned to the topic throughout his cross-examination. Carson also tried to justify Queensberry's characterisation by quoting from Wilde's novel, The Picture of Dorian Gray, referring in particular to a scene in the second chapter, in which Lord Henry Wotton explains his decadent philosophy to Dorian, an "innocent young man", in Carson's words.

Carson then moved to the factual evidence and questioned Wilde about his friendships with younger, lower-class men. Wilde admitted being on a first-name basis and lavishing gifts upon them, but insisted that nothing untoward had occurred and that the men were merely good friends of his. Carson repeatedly pointed out the unusual nature of these relationships and insinuated that the men were prostitutes. Wilde replied that he did not believe in social barriers, and simply enjoyed the society of young men. Then Carson asked Wilde directly whether he had ever kissed a certain servant boy, Wilde responded, "Oh, dear no. He was a particularly plain boy – unfortunately ugly – I pitied him for it." Carson pressed him on the answer, repeatedly asking why the boy's ugliness was relevant. Wilde hesitated, then for the first time became flustered: "You sting me and insult me and try to unnerve me; and at times one says things flippantly when one ought to speak more seriously."

In his opening speech for the defence, Carson announced that he had located several male prostitutes who were to testify that they had had sex with Wilde. On the advice of his lawyers, Wilde dropped the prosecution. Queensberry was found not guilty, as the court declared that his accusation that Wilde was "posing as a Somdomite " was justified, "true in substance and in fact".Under the Libel Act 1843, Queensberry's acquittal rendered Wilde legally liable for the considerable expenses Queensberry had incurred in his defence, which left Wilde bankrupt.

Regina v. Wilde

After Wilde left the court, a warrant for his arrest was applied for on charges of sodomy and gross indecency. Robbie Ross found Wilde at the Cadogan Hotel, Pont Street, Knightsbridge, with Reginald Turner; both men advised Wilde to go at once to Dover and try to get a boat to France; his mother advised him to stay and fight. Wilde, lapsing into inaction, could only say, "The train has gone. It's too late."On 6 April 1895, Wilde was arrested for "gross indecency" under Section 11 of the Criminal Law Amendment Act 1885, a term meaning homosexual acts not amounting to buggery (an offence under a separate statute). At Wilde's instruction, Ross and Wilde's butler forced their way into the bedroom and library of 16 Tite Street, packing some personal effects, manuscripts, and letters. Wilde was then imprisoned on remand at Holloway, where he received daily visits from Douglas.

Events moved quickly and his prosecution opened on 26 April 1895, before Mr Justice Charles. Wilde pleaded not guilty. He had already begged Douglas to leave London for Paris, but Douglas complained bitterly, even wanting to give evidence; he was pressed to go and soon fled to the Hotel du Monde. Fearing persecution, Ross and many others also left the United Kingdom during this time. Under cross examination Wilde was at first hesitant, then spoke eloquently:

Charles Gill (prosecuting): What is "the love that dare not speak its name"?

Wilde: "The love that dare not speak its name" in this century is such a great affection of an elder for a younger man as there was between David and Jonathan, such as Plato made the very basis of his philosophy, and such as you find in the sonnets of Michelangelo and Shakespeare. It is that deep spiritual affection that is as pure as it is perfect. It dictates and pervades great works of art, like those of Shakespeare and Michelangelo, and those two letters of mine, such as they are. It is in this century misunderstood, so much misunderstood that it may be described as "the love that dare not speak its name", and on that account of it I am placed where I am now. It is beautiful, it is fine, it is the noblest form of affection. There is nothing unnatural about it. It is intellectual, and it repeatedly exists between an older and a younger man, when the older man has intellect, and the younger man has all the joy, hope and glamour of life before him. That it should be so, the world does not understand. The world mocks at it, and sometimes puts one in the pillory for it.

This response was counter-productive in a legal sense as it only served to reinforce the charges of homosexual behaviour.

The trial ended with the jury unable to reach a verdict. Wilde's counsel, Sir Edward Clarke, was finally able to get a magistrate to allow Wilde and his friends to post bail. The Reverend Stewart Headlam put up most of the £5,000 surety required by the court, having disagreed with Wilde's treatment by the press and the courts. Wilde was freed from Holloway and, shunning attention, went into hiding at the house of Ernest and Ada Leverson, two of his firm friends. Edward Carson approached Frank Lockwood QC, the Solicitor General and asked "Can we not let up on the fellow now?"Lockwood answered that he would like to do so, but feared that the case had become too politicised to be dropped.

The final trial was presided over by Mr Justice Wills. On 25 May 1895 Wilde and Alfred Taylor were convicted of gross indecency and sentenced to two years' hard labour.The judge described the sentence, the maximum allowed, as "totally inadequate for a case such as this", and that the case was "the worst case I have ever tried". Wilde's response "And I? May I say nothing, my Lord?" was drowned out in cries of "Shame" in the courtroom.

Imprisonment

When first I was put into prison some people advised me to try and forget who I was. It was ruinous advice. It is only by realising what I am that I have found comfort of any kind. Now I am advised by others to try on my release to forget that I have ever been in a prison at all. I know that would be equally fatal. It would mean that I would always be haunted by an intolerable sense of disgrace, and that those things that are meant for me as much as for anybody else – the beauty of the sun and moon, the pageant of the seasons, the music of daybreak and the silence of great nights, the rain falling through the leaves, or the dew creeping over the grass and making it silver – would all be tainted for me, and lose their healing power, and their power of communicating joy. To regret one's own experiences is to arrest one's own development. To deny one's own experiences is to put a lie into the lips of one's own life. It is no less than a denial of the soul.

De Profundis

Wilde was incarcerated from 25 May 1895 to 18 May 1897.

He first entered Newgate Prison in London for processing, then was moved to Pentonville Prison, where the "hard labour" to which he had been sentenced consisted of many hours of walking a treadmill and picking oakum (separating the fibres in scraps of old navy ropes), and where prisoners were allowed to read only the Bible and The Pilgrim's Progress.

A few months later he was moved to Wandsworth Prison in London. Inmates there also followed the regimen of "hard labour, hard fare and a hard bed", which wore harshly on Wilde's delicate health. In November he collapsed during chapel from illness and hunger. His right ear drum was ruptured in the fall, an injury that later contributed to his death. He spent two months in the infirmary.

Richard B. Haldane, the Liberal MP and reformer, visited Wilde and had him transferred in November to Reading Gaol, 30 miles (48 km) west of London on 23 November 1895. The transfer itself was the lowest point of his incarceration, as a crowd jeered and spat at him on the railway platform. He spent the remainder of his sentence there, addressed and identified only as "C33" – the occupant of the third cell on the third floor of C ward.

About five months after Wilde arrived at Reading Gaol, Charles Thomas Wooldridge, a trooper in the Royal Horse Guards, was brought to Reading to await his trial for murdering his wife on 29 March 1896; on 17 June Wooldridge was sentenced to death and returned to Reading for his execution, which took place on Tuesday, 7 July 1896 – the first hanging at Reading in 18 years. From Wooldridge's hanging, Wilde later wrote The Ballad of Reading Gaol.

Wilde was not, at first, even allowed paper and pen but Haldane eventually succeeded in allowing access to books and writing materials. Wilde requested, among others: the Bible in French; Italian and German grammars; some Ancient Greek texts, Dante's Divine Comedy, Joris-Karl Huysmans's new French novel about Christian redemption En route, and essays by St Augustine, Cardinal Newman and Walter Pater.

Between January and March 1897 Wilde wrote a 50,000-word letter to Douglas. He was not allowed to send it, but was permitted to take it with him when released from prison. In reflective mode, Wilde coldly examines his career to date, how he had been a colourful agent provocateur in Victorian society, his art, like his paradoxes, seeking to subvert as well as sparkle. His own estimation of himself was: one who "stood in symbolic relations to the art and culture of my age". It was from these heights that his life with Douglas began, and Wilde examines that particularly closely, repudiating him for what Wilde finally sees as his arrogance and vanity: he had not forgotten Douglas' remark, when he was ill, "When you are not on your pedestal you are not interesting." Wilde blamed himself, though, for the ethical degradation of character that he allowed Douglas to bring about in him and took responsibility for his own fall, "I am here for having tried to put your father in prison." The first half concludes with Wilde forgiving Douglas, for his own sake as much as Douglas's. The second half of the letter traces Wilde's spiritual journey of redemption and fulfilment through his prison reading. He realised that his ordeal had filled his soul with the fruit of experience, however bitter it tasted at the time.

> ... I wanted to eat of the fruit of all the trees in the garden of the world ... And so, indeed, I went out, and so I lived. My only mistake was that I confined myself so exclusively to the trees of what seemed to me the sun-lit side of the garden, and shunned the other side for its shadow and its gloom.

Wilde was released from prison on 19 May 1897 and sailed that evening for Dieppe, France. He never returned to the UK.

On his release, he gave the manuscript to Ross, who may or may not have carried out Wilde's instructions to send a copy to Douglas (who later denied having received it). The letter was partially published in 1905 as De Profundis; its complete and correct publication first occurred in 1962 in The Letters of Oscar Wilde.

Decline: 1897–1900

Exile

Though Wilde's health had suffered greatly from the harshness and diet of prison, he had a feeling of spiritual renewal. He immediately wrote to the Society of Jesus requesting a six-month Catholic retreat; when the request was denied, Wilde wept. "I intend to be received into the Catholic Church before long", Wilde told a journalist who asked about his religious intentions.

He spent his last three years impoverished and in exile. He took the name "Sebastian Melmoth", after Saint Sebastian and the titular character of Melmoth the Wanderer (a Gothic novel by Charles Maturin, Wilde's great-uncle).Wilde wrote two long letters to the editor of the Daily Chronicle, describing the brutal conditions of English prisons and advocating penal reform. His discussion of the dismissal of Warder Martin for giving biscuits to an anaemic child prisoner repeated the themes of the corruption and degeneration of punishment that he had earlier outlined in The Soul of Man under Socialism.

Wilde spent mid-1897 with Robert Ross in the seaside village of Berneval-le-Grand in northern France, where he wrote The Ballad of Reading Gaol, narrating the execution of Charles Thomas Wooldridge, who murdered his wife in a rage at her infidelity. It moves from an objective story-telling to symbolic identification with the prisoners. No attempt is made to assess the justice of the laws which convicted them but rather the poem highlights the brutalisation of the punishment that all convicts share. Wilde juxtaposes the executed man and himself with the line "Yet each man kills the thing he loves". He adopted the proletarian ballad form and the author was credited as "C33", Wilde's cell number in Reading Gaol. He suggested that it be published in Reynolds' Magazine, "because it circulates widely among the criminal classes – to which I now belong – for once I will be read by my peers – a new experience for me". It was an immediate roaring commercial success, going through seven editions in less than two years, only after which "[Oscar" was added to the title page, though many in literary circles had known Wilde to be the author. It brought him a small amount of money.

Although Douglas had been the cause of his misfortunes, he and Wilde were reunited in August 1897 at Rouen. This meeting was disapproved of by the friends and families of both men. Constance Wilde was already refusing to meet Wilde or allow him to see their sons, though she sent him money – three pounds a week. During the latter part of 1897, Wilde and Douglas lived together near Naples for a few months until they were separated by their families under the threat of cutting off all funds.

Wilde's final address was at the dingy Hôtel d'Alsace (now known as L'Hôtel), on rue des Beaux-Arts in Saint-Germain-des-Prés, Paris. "This poverty really breaks one's heart: it is so sale , so utterly depressing, so hopeless. Pray do what you can" he wrote to his publisher.He corrected and published An Ideal Husband and The Importance of Being Earnest, the proofs of which, according to Ellmann, show a man "very much in command of himself and of the play" but he refused to write anything else: "I can write, but have lost the joy of writing".

He wandered the boulevards alone and spent what little money he had on alcohol. A series of embarrassing chance encounters with hostile English visitors, or Frenchmen he had known in better days, drowned his spirit. Soon Wilde was sufficiently confined to his hotel to joke, on one of his final trips outside, "My wallpaper and I are fighting a duel to the death. One of us has got to go". On 12 October 1900 he sent a telegram to Ross: "Terribly weak. Please come". His moods fluctuated; Max Beerbohm relates how their mutual friend Reginald 'Reggie' Turner had found Wilde very depressed after a nightmare. "I dreamt that I had died, and was supping with the dead!" "I am sure", Turner replied, "that you must have been the life and soul of the party."Turner was one of the few of the old circle who remained with Wilde to the end and was at his bedside when he died.

Death

By 25 November 1900 Wilde had developed meningitis, then called "cerebral meningitis". Robbie Ross arrived on 29 November, sent for a priest, and Wilde was conditionally baptised into the Catholic Church by Fr Cuthbert Dunne, a Passionist priest from Dublin,Wilde having been baptised in the Church of Ireland and having moreover a recollection of Catholic baptism as a child, a fact later attested to by the minister of the sacrament, Fr Lawrence Fox.Fr Dunne recorded the baptism,

> As the voiture rolled through the dark streets that wintry night, the sad story of Oscar Wilde was in part repeated to me... Robert Ross knelt by the bedside, assisting me as best he could while I administered conditional baptism, and afterwards answering the responses while I

gave Extreme Unction to the prostrate man and recited the prayers for the dying. As the man was in a semi-comatose condition, I did not venture to administer the Holy Viaticum; still I must add that he could be roused and was roused from this state in my presence. When roused, he gave signs of being inwardly conscious... Indeed I was fully satisfied that he understood me when told that I was about to receive him into the Catholic Church and gave him the Last Sacraments... And when I repeated close to his ear the Holy Names, the Acts of Contrition, Faith, Hope and Charity, with acts of humble resignation to the Will of God, he tried all through to say the words after me.

Wilde died of meningitis on 30 November 1900. Different opinions are given as to the cause of the disease: Richard Ellmann claimed it was syphilitic; Merlin Holland, Wilde's grandson, thought this to be a misconception, noting that Wilde's meningitis followed a surgical intervention, perhaps a mastoidectomy; Wilde's physicians, Dr Paul Cleiss and A'Court Tucker, reported that the condition stemmed from an old suppuration of the right ear (from the prison injury, see above) treated for several years (une ancienne suppuration de l'oreille droite d'ailleurs en traitement depuis plusieurs années) and made no allusion to syphilis.

Burial

Wilde was initially buried in the Cimetière de Bagneux outside Paris; in 1909 his remains were disinterred and transferred to Père Lachaise Cemetery, inside the city. His tomb there was designed by Sir Jacob Epstein. It was commissioned by Robert Ross, who asked for a small compartment to be made for his own ashes, which were duly transferred in 1950. The modernist angel depicted as a relief on the tomb was originally complete with male genitalia, which were initially censored by French Authorities with a golden leaf. The genitals have since been vandalised; their current whereabouts are unknown. In 2000, Leon Johnson, a multimedia artist, installed a silver prosthesis to replace them. In 2011, the tomb was cleaned of the many lipstick marks left there by admirers and a glass barrier was installed to prevent further marks or damage.

230

The epitaph is a verse from The Ballad of Reading Gaol,

And alien tears will fill for him

Pity's long-broken urn,

For his mourners will be outcast men,

And outcasts always mourn.

Posthumous pardon

In 2017, Wilde was among an estimated 50,000 men who were pardoned for homosexual acts that were no longer considered offences under the Policing and Crime Act 2017. The Act is known informally as the Alan Turing law.

Honours

In 2014 Wilde was one of the inaugural honorees in the Rainbow Honor Walk, a walk of fame in San Francisco's Castro neighbourhood noting LGBTQ people who have "made significant contributions in their fields."

Biographies

Wilde's life has been the subject of numerous biographies since his death. The earliest were memoirs by those who knew him: often they are personal or impressionistic accounts which can be good character sketches, but are sometimes factually unreliable. Frank Harris, his friend and editor, wrote a biography, Oscar Wilde: His Life and Confessions (1916); though prone to exaggeration and sometimes factually inaccurate, it offers a good literary portrait of Wilde. Lord Alfred Douglas wrote two books about his relationship with Wilde. Oscar Wilde and Myself (1914), largely ghost-written by T. W. H. Crosland, vindictively reacted to Douglas's discovery that De Profundis was addressed to him and defensively tried to distance him from Wilde's scandalous reputation. Both authors later regretted their work. Later, in Oscar Wilde: A Summing Up (1939) and his Autobiography he was more sympathetic to Wilde. Of Wilde's other close friends, Robert Sherard; Robert Ross, his literary executor; and Charles Ricketts variously published biographies, reminiscences or correspondence. The first more or less objective biography of Wilde came about when Hesketh Pearson wrote Oscar Wilde: His Life and Wit (1946). In 1954 Wilde's son Vyvyan Holland published his memoir Son of Oscar Wilde, which recounts the difficulties Wilde's wife and children faced after his imprisonment. It was revised and updated by Merlin Holland in 1989.

Oscar Wilde, a critical study by Arthur Ransome was published in 1912. The book only briefly mentioned Wilde's life, but subsequently Ransome (and The Times Book Club) were sued for libel by Lord Alfred Douglas. In April 1913 Douglas lost the libel action after a reading of De Profundis refuted his claims.

Richard Ellmann wrote his 1987 biography Oscar Wilde, for which he posthumously won a National (USA) Book Critics Circle Award in 1988and a Pulitzer Prize in 1989. The book was the basis for the 1997 film Wilde, directed by Brian Gilbert and starring Stephen Fry as the title character.

Neil McKenna's 2003 biography, The Secret Life of Oscar Wilde, offers an exploration of Wilde's sexuality. Often speculative in nature, it was widely criticised for its pure conjecture and lack of scholarly rigour. Thomas Wright's Oscar's Books (2008) explores Wilde's reading from his childhood in Dublin to his death in Paris. After tracking down many books that once belonged to Wilde's Tite Street library (dispersed at the time of his trials), Wright was the first to examine Wilde's marginalia.

Later on, I think everyone will recognise his achievements; his plays and essays will endure. Of course, you may think with others that his personality and conversation were far more wonderful than anything he wrote, so that his written works give only a pale reflection of his power. Perhaps that is so, and of course, it will be impossible to reproduce what is gone forever.

Robert Ross, 23 December 1900

In 2018, Matthew Sturgis' "Oscar: A Life," was published in London. The book incorporates rediscovered letters and other documents and is the most extensively researched biography of Wilde to appear since 1988.

Parisian literati, also produced several biographies and monographs on him. André Gide wrote In Memoriam, Oscar Wilde and Wilde also features in his journals. Thomas Louis, who had earlier translated books on Wilde into French, produced his own L'esprit d'Oscar Wilde in 1920. Modern books include Philippe Jullian's Oscar Wilde, and L'affaire Oscar Wilde, ou, Du danger de laisser la justice mettre le nez dans nos draps (The Oscar Wilde Affair, or, On the Danger of Allowing Justice to put its Nose in our Sheets) by Odon Vallet, a French religious historian. (Source: Wikipedia)

NOTABLE WORKS

ESSAYS

"The Decay of Lying" First published in Nineteenth Century (1889), republished in Intentions (1891).

"Pen, Pencil and Poison" First published in the Fortnightly Review (1889), republished in Intentions (1891).

"The Soul of Man under Socialism" First published in the Fortnightly Review (1891), republished in The Soul of Man (1895), privately printed.

Intentions (1891) Wilde revised his dialogues on aesthetic subjects for publication in this volume, which comprises:

- "The Critic as Artist"
- "The Decay of Lying"
- "Pen, Pencil and Poison"
- "The Truth of Masks"

"Phrases and Philosophies for the Use of the Young" first published in the Oxford student magazine The Chameleon, December 1894)

"A Few Maxims For The Instruction Of The Over-Educated" First published, anonymously, in the 1894 November 17 issue of Saturday Review.

FICTION

Novel

The Picture of Dorian Gray (1890/1891). The first version of "The Picture of Dorian Gray" was published, in a form highly edited by the magazine, as the lead story in the July 1890 edition of Lippincott's Monthly Magazine. Wilde published the longer and revised version in book form in 1891, with an added preface.

Stories

"The Portrait of Mr. W. H." (1889)

The Happy Prince and Other Tales (1888, a collection of fairy tales) consisting of:

- "The Happy Prince"

- "The Nightingale and the Rose"

- "The Selfish Giant"

- "The Devoted Friend"

- "The Remarkable Rocket"

A House of Pomegranates (1891, fairy tales)

Lord Arthur Savile's Crime and Other Stories (1891) Including "The Canterville Ghost" first published in periodical form in 1887.

Complete Short Fiction. Penguin Classics, 2003. Edited with an Introduction and Notes by Ian Small. Contains all works listed above plus Poems in Prose (1894) and one very short 'Elder-tree' (fragment).

POEMS

Ravenna (1878) Winner of the Newdigate Prize.

Poems (1881) Wilde's collection of poetry and first publication.

The Sphinx (1894)

Poems in Prose (1894)

The Ballad of Reading Gaol (1898)

PLAYS

Vera; or, The Nihilists (1880)

The Duchess of Padua (1883)

Lady Windermere's Fan (1892)

A Woman of No Importance (1893)

Salomé (French version) (1893, first performed in Paris 1896)

Salomé: A Tragedy in One Act: Translated from the French of Oscar Wilde by Lord Alfred Douglas, illustrated by Aubrey Beardsley (1894)

An Ideal Husband (1895) (text)

The Importance of Being Earnest (1895) (text)

La Sainte Courtisane and A Florentine Tragedy Fragmentary. First published 1908 in Methuen's Collected Works

(Dates are dates of first performance, which approximate better to the probable date of composition than dates of publication.)

The Importance of Being Earnest and Other Plays. Penguin Classics, 2000. Edited with an Introduction, Commentaries and Notes by Richard Allen Cave. Contains all from above save the first two. Salome is in English.

As an appendix there is one excised scene from The Importance of Being Earnest.

POSTHUMOUS (PREVIOUSLY UNPUBLISHED)

De Profundis (Written 1895-97, in Reading Gaol). Expurgated edition published 1905; suppressed portions 1913, expanded version in The Letters of Oscar Wilde (1962).

The Rise of Historical Criticism (Written while at college) First published in 1905 (Sherwood Press, Hartford, CT) privately printed. Reprinted in Miscellanies, the last volume of the First Collected Edition (1908).

The First Collected Edition (Methuen & Co., 14 volumes) appeared in 1908 and contained many previously unpublished works.

The Second Collected Edition (Methuen & Co., 12 volumes) appeared in installments between 1909–11 and contained several other unpublished works.

The Letters of Oscar Wilde (Written 1868-1900) Published in 1962. Republished as The Complete Letters of Oscar Wilde (2000), with letters discovered since 1962, and new annotations by Merlin Holland.

The Women of Homer (Written 1876, while at college). First published in Oscar Wilde: The Women of Homer (2008) by The Oscar Wilde Society.

The Philosophy of Dress First published in The New-York Tribune (1885), published for the first time in book form in Oscar Wilde On Dress (2013).

MISATTRIBUTED

Teleny, or The Reverse of the Medal (Paris, 1893) has been attributed to Wilde, but its authorship is unclear. One theory is that it was a combined effort by several of Wilde's friends, which he may have edited.

Constance On September 14, 2011, Wilde's grandson Merlin Holland contested Wilde's claimed authorship of this play entitled Constance, scheduled to open that week in the King's Head Theatre. It was not, in fact, "Oscar Wilde's final play," as its producers were claiming. Holland said Wilde did sketch out the play's scenario in 1894, but "never wrote a word" of it, and that "it is dishonest to foist this on the public." The Artistic Director Adam Spreadbury-Maher of the King's Head Theatre and producer of Constance pointed out that Wilde's son, Vyvyan Holland, wrote in 1954, "a significant amount of the dialogue (of Constance) bears the authentic stamp of my father's hand". There is further proof that the developed scenario that Constance was reconstituted from was written by Wilde between 1897 and his death in 1900, rather than the 1894 George Alexander scenario which Merlin Holland quotes.

CPSIA information can be obtained
at www.ICGtesting.com
Printed in the USA
LVHW010013180820
663425LV00003B/316